DEADLY 21ST CENTURY

Charles L. (Bud) Evans

Contents

CHARLES L (BUD) EVANS

INTRODUCTION

This book is truly about surviving. It is not supposed to have all of the information that you will need to survive and succeed in the 21 first century. Here is a little information about me. I am a 71 year old redneck from Montana at the time that I am writing this. I will always be a redneck but I might be older when you read this. Here are my qualifications in brief: Raised in Central Montana, Judith Gap to be exact. Graduated from Montana State College, Bozeman, in chemistry education, with a minor in industrial arts. Masters Degree in science from Fort Wright College of Holy Names, now Heritage College, with a major in biology and a minor in physical science.

- Taught high school science for 6 years.
- Ran an auto repair business and wrecking yard for about 15 years.
- Worked for the United States Navy as a radiation protection technician for two years.
- Spent 13 years on the Hanford Nuclear Reservation as a Senior Health Physicist.
- Written 12 Kindle books.
- Graduated from the COLLEGE OF HARD KNOCK with d's for doing.

I have been through enough trials to know what it takes to get through life. I have failed more than anybody I know. I also have tried more things than anybody in my acquaintances. This qualifies me to write a book on how to succeed and survive the 21st century.

You might find some of my statements in this book objectionable. Okay, you don't agree, take the good stuff and leave the rest. This is a beginning book, not a bible on how to survive.

I have a PhD from the School of Hard Knocks. We have been through the following disasters:

- Bankrupt due to health reasons.
- Burned out by fire twice
- House fire in Shelton, Washington
- Hanford Fire of 2000 from Hanford Nuclear Reservation $250,000 loss.
- Put out of business by Benton County on a change of zoning applications.
- Fired from a $100K per year job because I would not lie for the government or their contractors.
- Assessed unreasonable rates by the local irrigation district while on a fixed income.

My education and experience provide the knowledge to write this book. Many parts of this guide will be from other papers and books that I have written. This will not be a complete guide on survival but it will be the best that I can provide based upon my knowledge. This book is based upon the best knowledge available at the time of writing. Any information that you use and implement is your choice and the outcome is your responsibility.

Charles L. (Bud) Evans

DEDICATION

This book is dedicated to my Parents that did a good job. My Mother taught me to garden and my Dad taught me to work hard. These are two things that are missing from the education of most of today's youth *This book is dedicated to my Mother, Florence I Evans. She was truly a master gardener to produce the amount of food that she did in those mountain gardens. Mom was old school with a lot of the old German level of expectation in her genes. There was only one way to do something and that was the right way, period end of statement. This was how she approached gardening both for food and for beauty. Thanks Mom for your love and toughness.*

Disclaimers and Legal Stuff

Copyright and Disclaimer Information

This is not meant to be a comprehensive guide to emergency preparedness but rather a starting point. Do your research and do the work to be prepared.

THE MISSION OF THIS BOOK

The mission of this book is to get you started on the path to self sufficiency. The definition of self sufficiency will be yours and you must define it for yourself and your family. This book is not about guns and ammo but rather about doing those things that will allow you to survive in nearly any situation. It definitely is not about revolution but with the current conditions in the United States that is a possibility.

CHAPTER 1
THE LIST

The Following Listed Items are must do items to survive in the world as we know it today 2012 and the world that we will live in, in the years to come.

- One year supply of non-perishable food stored.
- Get out of debt—do it now.
- Have a year's supply of clothing and don't forget good durable shoes.
- Maintain good health and store needed medications where possible.
- Maintain a positive and cheerful attitude; most of the events that will affect your life occurred beyond your control.
- Develop good community relations.
- Inventory your skills and develop new ones that you need.
- If possible store a year's supply of energy for cooking, light and heat.
- Store a year's supply of domestic animal feed.
- Get land to grow your own food.
- Develop strong spiritual beliefs and accept the guidance given.
- Develop a time management plan to get everything done.
- Study and research alternative medical treatments.
- Develop some type of home security plan.
- Consider the ultimate disaster.
- Put together a "Bug out Kit".

Some updates for October 2013.

- Today we had a shutdown of government with a few exceptions. The military and Social Security and a couple of other needs will still be paid. I am sure that Congress and the President will still get their checks. This creates a new need to have a stash of emergency cash available.
- The folks responsible for documenting climatic change have agreed that global warming is inevitable and it was cause by hydrocarbon emission. This just is not true. Many of the indicators based upon eons of geological data paint a different picture. We have had current events that will cause more climatic change than global warming. The greatest of these is the shift of the earth's axis and the level of energy emitted from the sun. The actual energy received by the Earth from the sun is decreasing. We are headed for global cooling not global warming. This being said I would add a family greenhouse to the list of things necessary for long term survival.

These are the basics to survive many more can be added. This book will address these items. Many other needed items will be addressed as resources.

CHARLES L (BUD) EVANS

CHAPTER 2
IS SELF-SUFFICIENT LIVING FOR YOU?

Many people look at self sufficient living as being away from society. That is a matter of definition and it depends upon what you want. Do you really want to be away from everyone else? To live self sufficiently is that necessary?

Let's look at self sufficiency. I believe that self sufficiency is attainable in degrees. Where I grew up in the Mountains of Montana self sufficiency was a way of life. It did not exclude the rest of the world. Today to be totally self sufficient is a pipe dream of the first order. You will always need something from someone else, whether it is parts for your machinery or cloth to make clothes. (A little ice cream on occasion is good too.) Yes nearly all of these things can be produced at home, however, that might not be the best way to be self sufficient.

Sometimes being self sufficient is being able to barter your skills with someone that has a skill in a different area. Trading grain for hay to feed your livestock does not make you less self sufficient. You need to decide what self sufficiency means to you. It means these things to me:

- As totally self sufficient in all areas of my life that I can reasonably be. (The key word is reasonable.)
- No outside financial help is a must. This means that I will make all of my own expenses, preferably at home on my land.
- Produce as much of our own food as possible.
- Produce as much of our own energy as possible.

- Achieve financial independence.
- Adequate housing and land for my family.
- The ability to survive for one year with minimal outside supplies.
- Neighborhood relationships that allow everyone to survive in a crisis.

Now I need to choose where I am going to set up my homestead. My personal choice is a small rural community with land not too far from a near small town. Where I grew up it was 1/4 of a mile to the nearest neighbor and the next neighbor was 5 miles away. It was 15 miles by dirt road to town. I don't want that life style today even though it was fun as a child.

CHARLES L (BUD) EVANS

CHAPTER 3
HOW TO MAKE IT HAPPEN

Your current question is how I can put all of those things in that checklist together. They cost too much, will take to much time and I don't know how. The first step is accomplishing any long term or for that matter immediate project is to make a plan. I have included some excerpts from one of my books to help you along. The best way to start any plan is to define where you want to be when you get it done. The idea is to start with the end in mind and work backwards until you reach where you are today. The final step is to have the patience to work you plan. The sections that follow should help you get started.

"This author believes that there are three basic steps to success. This process has been proven over and over again by many successful persons.

- Prayer
- Planning
- Persistence

These are the three P's of success. Each is important in its own place. The first, Prayer I leave up to the individual and his own beliefs. The second, I will address to some extent. The third Persistence is determined by the individual.

HOW TO MAKE A PLAN

There are a lot of methods used to formulate a plan. The simplest method and the method that I use is called backward planning. In the simplest form this is visualizing the end result and then deciding what the previous step to get to the final step was. You now have two steps in your plan. Now you take a step backward, what do I need to do to accomplish this level?

This is a simple method but it requires one thing. You need to know where you want to end. If you don't know your objective then backward planning won't work.

My personal opinion is to look into ourselves and see what we really want out of life. Most people seem to want the same things in the core of their being. For most it is something like this. Family and companionship, financial security, meaningful work or service, and leisure activities that are meaningful to the individual.

I will share my core values with you. My great passions in life are:

- Family
- Service
- Fixing things
- Gardening
- Learning and the internet.

My goals from these are fairly simple but not so easy to obtain. My passion for my family breaks down into many areas. Some are:

- Financial
- Friendship and relationships
- Legacy
- Tradition

The other areas can be broken down into many smaller pieces also. One similar point in all of these personal passions is a financial piece. Everything that we do must be funded in

CHARLES L (BUD) EVANS

some manner and that leads us to financial planning and managing our money.

I am not going to get into the intricate subject of financial planning from the stand point of stocks, bonds, real estate and other investments as these are just one part on managing your money.

Your financial plan begins with goals. What do you really want? How much will it cost? This author has one piece of advice. Don't cut down your dream to match your budget. Make your budget match your dream.

This is easier to do than you think and the steps are practically the same.

Find out where you are financially. This requires that you develop a financial statement. This will include all assets and all liabilities. (What you own and what you owe.) It will include all saving and all loans.

Evaluate your income and expenses. This will eventually lead to a budget however you can develop a budget without any information. The evaluation is accomplished by tracking and this many times proves to be the most difficult part. Tracking is just that. Track all of your income and expenditures. My suggestion is to get a small pocket notebook for each member of the family. Children about 8 years old should do this too. In this note book write down everything you spend. Even include that 25 cents for a piece of gum from the machine. Record the amount and what you purchased or spent the money on. Do the same for all income. Write down your gross income and write down any deductions as expenses. In other words track your income and expenses. Businesses go to great lengths with complicated computer programs to do this.

Develop a budget or spending plan from this information. A budget is nothing more than a plan of how you are going to spend your money.

Develop a savings plan. Ten percent of your take home income should be placed in saving. I believe that we should live on 80% of our take home or spendable income. Spendable income for this use is that income after taxes generally income tax, social security and insurance.

Figure out a method to pay your bill and expenses on 80% of your gross income. You will have to make major adjustments to do this. One individual had three new cars and was making over $2500 per month car payments. This family decided that one good family car with a couple of old clunkers made better sense. This took a little time but they cut their car payments by $1500 per month. This adjustment by itself wiped out their negative balance each month that was ending up on credit cards.

CHARLES L (BUD) EVANS

CHAPTER 4
THE 3 P'S OF SUCCESS

This action requires contemplation and personal thought. I don't expect you to take everything here as the whole truth and nothing but the truth. Use the grocery store method, "If you can use it take it home with you." Don't condemn the whole book just because you don't agree with one statement.

THE THREE P'S

I have learned by the school of hard knocks that there are three things necessary to succeed in any endeavor. They are:

- Prayer
- Planning
- Persistence

I am not sure if there is any certain order that these P's should be applied. Persistence is always the last one. You must persist until you succeed. You must plan to know how to persist. God's help in necessary for all of these to happen so Prayer comes at all levels.

PRAYER

What is prayer? Many people believe that prayer is a method of communications. I know that this is true. In my belief system I know that I can communicate with God through prayer. Prayer can take many forms, for some it might be mediation or pondering a thought for others it may be more formal but it is always a way to communicate with a higher form of intelligence.

Prayer provides me with a consulting service on any challenge. I once had a friend go to my Bishop asking what was wrong with me.

He said, "That Evans prays and thinks he gets answers."

My Bishop answered. "We all have our problems but I wouldn't worry about his."

It is useless to pray and not expect to get an answer. Faith is part of the process of prayer. If you don't expect an answer, why pray in the first place. I get answers but not always the ones that I want. Prayer and faith are an essential part of the equation for success. This author can't tell you what you must do; however, you must find your own direction and method to communicate with God or some higher form of intelligence.

PLANNING

Planning is an essential part of any action. Even simple actions require a plan. Sometimes the plan is to do nothing and let our actions be directed by the events as they take place. A plan has not been constructed but a choice has been made. Planning is selecting options that we believe will get us to a certain goal.

Planning does not begin with the project that we are working on. Planning begins with deciding what we want to be and what we want to do with our lives. Each individual needs to determine his own destiny. Each must decide his own direction.

My method of planning a life is to develop a mission statement. You asked, "What is a mission statement?" A mission statement is what you are. A good friend of mine who has now passed through the veil put it this way. "It doesn't matter what a man does or what a man say, what is important is what a

24

man is." What he meant was that no matter how much good you do if you do it for the wrong reason it is unimportant. What you are and what you believe is what is important. My definition of a mission statement is a verbal description of what you are, what you want to be and how you are going to get there.

Writing and developing a mission statement will be one of the hardest thing you have ever done. It will be worth the effort. I spent three years developing my mission statement and since it was finished I have changed 25 words in three pages. My mission statement was completed over 15 years ago. My life had little meaning until I completed the mission statement. A mission statement is not an unchangeable document, however it should be changed with great care once that it is complete. The world evolves and your mission statement must be kept up to date. If your mission statement is written on correct principles the changes will be few. This paper is an extension of my mission statement and will help me to achieve one of the goals set forth in my mission statement.

The statement that this book will help me to bring to reality is:

"SERVICE: I will help at least 1,000,000 people to approach their physical, spiritual, financial, mental and social potential."

The best sources of information on developing a mission statement are provided by Stephen R. Covey in THE SEVEN HABITS OF HIGHLY EFFECTIVE PEOPLE and in PUT FIRST THINGS FIRST.

Any plan that you make must be consistent with your mission statement. Each of us must make our lives consistent. All of the elements must balance. In order to develop a plan for any project or goal you must know where you want to go and

25

why you want to get there. The current plan must be evaluated against your core values.

If you do not ensure that what you are planning is part of your core value system you will not succeed and if you do it will not be the most pleasant process. Happiness and success work together. They are not mutually exclusive but rather are interlocked. Love your work and you will not work another day in your life. This means do what is consistent with your core values and your mission statement and you will be happy, successful and life will be good.

BARBRA SHER'S BOOK

Barbara Sher wrote a book called: **WISHCRAFT, HOW TO GET WHAT YOU REALLY WANT.** This is one of the best books on practical self-help that I have ever read. I have recommended it to a lot of people and all thought it was a great help.

This book will help you discover who your are and what you want to do when you grow up. **WISHCRAFT** is a big help in developing a mission statement.

ASSIGNMENT ONE

Your first assignment is to develop a mission statement. Take the time to do the reading and the research. Look into the very bottom of your soul and discover your true values and worth.

SOME PLANNING METHODS

The method of planning that I like is to start at the end point and work backwards in steps. This provides general outline of what we need to reach a goal. The best explanation of this type of planning is in a book by Barbara Sher, titled WISHCRAFT.

26

CHARLES L (BUD) EVANS

Dr. Steven Covey stated that we must begin with the end in mind. I am a firm believer in this thought. To begin with the end in mind we must first determine what is the end. The end result becomes our goal. After we have established the goal then we take a small step backward from the goal and visualize what the step taken before the goal would be. After we determine that step we step back a little more and repeat the process. This process is continued until we get back to our present situation. Many times the steps that we must take are not apparent. When the next step back is not apparent it is time to do some research. Today the Internet, libraries and friends are all available to help.. In fact many times the research is the next step back.

That last paragraph was a lot of impossible tasks for the average person without a place to start. If you don't have a fair idea of what you want and where to start, develop a mind map. What is a mind map? A mind map is a method to develop and organize your thoughts about a single subject.

How do you create a mind map? There probably is not one better method than the other but I start with a blank sheet of paper preferably without lines or borders (I use an artist sketch pad.). In the center of the page I print the subject that needs to be brainstormed. Then I draw a circle around the subject.

If mind mapping is your bag here are couple of books to help. <u>MINDMAPPING</u> by Joyce Wycoff and <u>USE BOTH SIDES OF YOUR BRAIN</u> by Tony Buzan. These are two older books on the subject but they are still great information

A mindmap does not have to be a thing of great beauty. Mine are not. I have seen mindmaps that should have been framed and hung in an art gallery or a museum.

On lines that radiate out from the center are placed main thoughts. Along these lines are specific ideas and tasks, the big

27

thing is that these mind maps need to be fun. I get a great gob of colored pens and use them to organize specific ideas. When I get done I draw lines around related ideas.

You might ask why not just make an outline. Don't know the answer to that one. Mind maps just work better for me. When writing procedures I drew mind maps and could produce an acceptable procedure in a third the time it took when I used an outline.

Mind mapping is really a form of brainstorming that we can do as an individual or in a group. It is a great way to record and organize the thoughts of a group. Mindmapping allows us to use both sides of our brain.

After we have a plan to get to the end we must take the first step. Many times the steps will changes as we develop the path to our goal but we still have a plan. The plan should not be considered to be "Set in Concrete."

After we have developed a "mental" plan then it needs to be put on paper. I like flow charts. Again I don't follow all of the rules for rigorous flow charting technique. My flowcharts work for me and provide a guide for me.

The Kindle version of this book has some examples of mind maps but I could not get the resolution high enough to include them.

PERSISTENCE

The third P is persistence. This is the hard one to define but it mean simply keeping on until the goal is achieved. If we have a passion for and want our goal bad enough we will do what it takes to get to the end result. I must say that all steps must be taken with honesty and integrity. If we do not achieve our end

CHARLES L (BUD) EVANS

result using correct principles then the end result will be meaningless to us.

I know of one businessman that applied for a loan at over sixty lenders before he received the money necessary to fund his business. The point is he kept going until the desired result was achieved.

I believe that these three P's if properly applied will allow you to accomplish anything.

PATIENCE

Patience may well be the fourth **P** of success. This will not be voiced too loudly as this author does not rate very high in this area. In all things it takes time to get results and I want things to happen now. A good friend suggested that I include patience as the fourth P of success and I think that she is right.

The How for survival starts with three basic things?

- To survive you must have food, water and shelter.
- To have an adequate supply of food stored you must have organized your finances to get that food supply.
- You will need to develop a plan to get that year's supply. It won't happen overnight but it still can be accomplished.

Gardening and sound financial management will be large steps in getting a year's supply of food. I won't attempt to tell you how to garden in this checklist. There are several excellent references about gardening in the resource section. I will give you information on how to construct a sim-

ple and productive garden. If I get carried away please for-
give me as I love to garden.

CHARLES L (BUD) EVANS

CHAPTER 5
A YEAR'S SUPPLY OF FOOD.

I have stolen the chapter on food storage from the book FOOD STORAGE AND PRESERVATION to include here as an introduction to storing food.

"My suggestion is that you need to store enough food, clothes, fuel and medical supplies for one year, at least. I know that this is not always possible as in some places it is illegal or there is just no room to store that amount. The largest problem that always arises is how I afford that much food. This is again a matter of preparation.

This book is only going to address food storage and preservation with a few suggestions of other things to store. Here are some priority items to store and obtain:

You should store what you family will eat. There are a few exceptions to this rule but generally store what you eat. This will allow a rotational plan that will always keep your stores fresh.

Where possible you should store food that does not require refrigeration. We have experiences some extended power outages in this county. If the temperature is in the 60 to 100 degree range frozen food in a freezer even if it is not opened will not last more than a few days.

You should have a generator to run your freeze and a few other appliances if possible. If you live in the city in an apartment this probably would not be possible. If you have a generator you will also need fuel for it.

It is recommended that you store one year's supply of wheat. This can be ground to flour and wheat has a long storage life. This will require that you have a wheat grinder. You should look for one that can be driven either by electricity and also cranked by hand. A general recommendation is that you have about 300 pounds of wheat for each member of your family.

Most of us are carnivores. We like meat. Fresh meat is a problem to store and the only way to store it is in a freezer. Wheat will provide you with enough protein in a pinch. Meat can be canned and stored. Canned tuna is a good storage item. I can't tell you how much but if you have a family food budget that should give you a good indication of how much meat product you need to store. Another way to store meat is live animals such as chickens and rabbit. If you have the room this is an excellent way to get meat for your food storage. Don't forget to store animal feed.

Vegetables are hard to store fresh. Most vegetables can well without a great loss of nutrient in the process. Many vegetables can be dried for long term storage. My recommendation is to have at least three serving a day of vegetable for every member of your family for one year. How do I afford that many vegetables? I suggest that you grow a garden if possible. Small raised beds can be integrated into any lawn or flower garden. We will cover raising vegetables in some depth later but here is a good book on vegetable gardening. Most of this book will be included: VEGETABLE GARDENING FOR FOOD PRODUCTION AND SELF SUFFICIENCY.

Feed for your animals and pets. Many pets can be feed table scraps and kept alive and well. You should plan for food for you animals and pets as well as for yourself.

Do you need to store fuel to heat your house if the power goes out for an extended period in the winter? The answer to this is yes. How do I do this? This is a question that will require

32

you to search for the best answer to meet your needs. Believe it or not I am still struggling with this problem especially in the changing economic times.

In some areas air conditioning is necessary. This can be particularly trying for the elderly. Plan ahead to cool your home without the power grid.

Do you have a plan to obtain adequate water during an emergency? Water storage is a must. For a long term water supply you might need to use your own ingenuity.

It is necessary to store first aid supplies to meet your needs. Those with special medical conditions should store those items require to meet these needs.

If you live in the Amazon jungle storing clothing might not be necessary but for the rest of us it is. Store those clothes that you will wear. As time goes on make sure that the sizes are correct. Be sure to store work clothes as they will meet many situations especially those that arise from disaster and loss of a job.

The greatest thing that can be done to protect your family during times of stress is to be debt free. You should not owe any money except for your home and your land. These should be paid off as soon as possible. Take it from one that has had to deal with debt that debt free is the best answer.

One thing that many folks don't have are garden seeds. Store garden seeds. You can now buy viable non-hybrid open pollinated seeds in a sealed can. They should be good for at least 5 years if kept at a moderate temperature.

The question now arises, how much should I store? You ought to store enough to meet your family's needs for a year. This is not an easy question to answer but I will try to provide some guide lines.

These are the basic items and you should expand them from this point. Please see the resource page for additional resources.

Item	Amount/person	Comments
Grain, wheat, rice	300lb	
Non-fat dried milk	75lb	Must be rotated
Sugar or Honey	60lb	
Salt	5lb	
Fat or oils	20lb	Canola, Lard, veb.
Dried Legumes	60lb	Beans, Peas, etc
Garden Seeds	Enough to replace food supply	Open Pollinated seed
Water	2 weeks/person = 14 gallons	
Bedding	Enough to keep everyone warm	
Clothes	A year's supply	Plan on changing sizes. Be smart store the clothes that you will wear.
Medical	As necessary	
Fuel and Lighting	A years supply	
Emergency Cash	Enough to meet 6 months expenses	

You will notice that the table did not list any meats. This does not mean that meat is not nice. It is great, however, there are only three ways to store meat and all of them are not easy. 1) You can store meat as live animals and butcher them as you need the meat. 2) It can be stored in a freezer and I know one

34

CHARLES L (BUD) EVANS

family that has four freezes full of food and two backup generators to keep them going in a crisis. 3) Meat may be canned. Canning meat requires that you follow all the precautions to ensure that it does not spoil in the container as spoiled meat can go unnoticed and kill you even if it is cooked after it is opened. It is your responsibility to determine if and how you will store meat for your family.

Store garden seeds, Just Do It!

CHAPTER 6
HOW TO GET STUFF

This is really the question most people ask. I can just barely balance my budget now. How can I afford to store food? Can you afford to not store food? The real question is do you really have a realistic budget. Enough said about that. You can access help with your budget in the appendix. If you put your mind to it you can find the things that you need to store. If you start then the opportunities to get what you need will come.

How do I get food to store?

Whenever you buy groceries buy an extra can. For example say that you buy 6 can of soup. Buy 7 everybody can afford that. If you do that every time you buy soup you soon will have a few cans in storage. Just add soup to your grocery list when your inventory gets down to you stored size. This is a simple concept but over time it will build food storage.

Grow a garden and can or freeze what you don't eat. Our goal this year is to produce more than 50 percent of our own food. Most of this will come from our garden.

Contact organizations that promote food storage such as the LDS Church.

Shop the internet for dried or canned food items sometime things show up on eBay and Craig's list.

Ask your family to give you food storage items for gifts.

Check out any neighbors that are moving. Many times they can't move their food or they don't want to.

If you have a place to do it raise your own live stock. Chickens and rabbits can be raised most any place.

Follow the local produce markets as sometime you can get great value here.

What can I store for fuel and light? This is a difficult question and is dependent upon where you live. If you live in the woods or heat your home with a wood stove this becomes easier. Just keep a year's supply of dry wood ahead and you have the fuel to heat your home. If you are lucky enough to have a wood cook stove then you fuel problem is solved.

If you don't have a source of heat such as wood then there are other alternatives. A pellet stove is a pretty good way to store heat for you house. It will require a battery backup with an inverter for power. Pellets can be easily and safely stored in a shed or garage. If you can afford it a solar powered charger can be use to charge the battery to run the pellet stove. Cooking fuel is another matter. Here are a few solutions for cooking: In the summer in most areas you can use solar reflectors as a solar oven to cook your food. You will have to do your own research in this area as I don't have a proven method. I do know several people that have used this method successfully.

Propane with a good camp stove can be a solution to cooking your food. **WARNING:** Propane is an explosive gas. Propane should not be stored in any living area or even in your garage if it is attached to your house. Three or four 8 gallon propane tanks will provide a couple of months of cooking fuel if use sparingly. Use your own judgment on how much you want to store. These are about the only alternatives for cooking other than cooking over an open fire. This works but is not the best solution in most areas.

For light I recommend camping lanterns and solar powered LED lights. The camping lanterns can be fueled either with portable propane cylinders or be gasoline/lantern fuel burning

CHARLES L (BUD) EVANS

lanterns. Please remember that storage of lantern fuel should meet the same requirements as storage of gasoline.

A backup generator is as almost always a must for rural settings and sometimes for other home sites. How can I afford a backup generator? Check Craig's list and eBay or Amazon for bargains. The first thing to decide is how large a generator you need. Figure out your critical uses for electricity. Some things to look at are:

- Well pump
- Pellet stove
- Recharging batteries
- Freezers and refrigerators

Find out what the power requirements for each of the units are. Remember that motors such as pumps require a lot more amperage for starting than for running. You must have a large enough generator to start the largest electric motor that an emergency might require. Generally you can alternate running different machines at different times to compensate for lack of gross power.

In summary you can obtain the items you need to store by being watchful for sales, people moving and yard sales. Be frugal with your emergency preparedness and storage money.

What clothes should I store and where can I get them. Many times you can obtain clothes at the thrift shop for storage. I believe that all families ought to be shopping the thrift shops for children's clothes anyway. If the thrift shop has clothes that fit you and they are something that you will wear then this is a good place to get adult clothes also. Remember that children clothes size change a lot in a year. Try to be proactive and buy good quality but inexpensive clothes for your children while estimating how much they will grow in a year.

Hand me down are a great way to meet your children's clothing needs. These can be your own family or even friends and neighbors. Start a neighborhood clothes sharing group. Don't forget Craig's List and eBay

.

CHAPTER 7
GARDENING 203

No book about home storage and beginning preparedness would be complete without a chapter on gardening. Today about 80 percent of the cost of our food is energy related either in the production stage or transporting the food to our homes. Home canning of a case of home grown produce can save as barrel of imported oil. Gardening is not a difficult thing to do. You can grow a very productive garden in a relatively small space. Even most apartment dwellers can grow some food in containers. Every little bit helps the environment and the economy as well as you bottom line.

RAISED BED INTENSIVE GARDEN: HOW TO BUILD ONE FOR SELF SUFFICIENCY

What is this section? It is a guide to grow more of our own food as easily as possible. It contains instructions and directions to accomplish that goal. Basically I am a lazy person. Do something once, do it right and enjoy the benefits. This is the secret of intensive bed gardening. They are more work in the beginning but require less work later on.

I will show you how to build beds and care for them. I cannot show you how to grow a garden. You must learn that for yourself.

This book is not intended to be the end all of gardening books. It is a place to start with raised bed gardening. My focus is to grow the most food with the least long term effort. You can make your garden beautiful. I just don't have the time. We don't claim that you will grow food like we do. Each garden produces according to the efforts and the love of the owner.

WHAT IS AN INTENSIVE RAISED BED GARDEN?

A raised bed garden is just that. It is a small bed maybe 5 feet wide by 5 feet long. The bed is constructed to provide maximum growth attributed to the plants. The nutrition is right, the correct amount of light is present, the soil temperature is okay, and the bed always has the correct amount of water.

Intensive bed gardening has been around for a long time. There is evidence that this method of gardening existed in ancient Egypt during the Israelite enslavement. Some researchers have found evidence of this type of farming in the Late Classic Maya cultures around 300 to 900 AD. There is historical relic in the American Southwest that shows the use of intensive bed farming on a fairly large scale. My question is why it took so long for people to recognize this very effective way of growing food.

The present day evolution of intensive bed gardening is attributed to Chadwick of the University of California, Santa Cruz. He took a barren hillside and through the use of what he called French intensive gardening turned it in to a lush hillside full of produce and flowers. John Jeavons continue with his work on another campus. John Jeavons has written several books on the subject.

So what is an intensive raised bed garden and why is it call intensive. It is a constructed bed, usually with sides made of some rot resistant material that is filled with those things that plants like to have to grow the best. The bed can be tailored to a specific plant. I have successfully used this method for field

42

CHARLES L (BUD) EVANS

gardening, however, the word intense takes on a new meaning when using this method in large plots without walls to contain the beds. These are a lot of work.

My beds are generally built out of scrap materials. The ones that I am constructing this year use old metal building siding that was given to me and some old treated 2 X 4 for stakes to hold them together. This is a typical raised bed.

The construction of a raised bed is simple. It is a fair amount of work. Make sure that you corner and side stakes are secure as they hold the weight of the dirt. Sometime it is necessary to frame the top of the bed with 2 X 4s. This will hold the sides.

PLAN YOUR GARDEN

Planning your garden is important. It is important because a well thought out plan makes construction and maintenance easier. Here are a few things that you must consider when planning your garden:

What are the total dimensions of your garden area? Make a scaled drawing of where you want to put your garden. That means measure it, don't just sketch it out.

Decide what you want to grow in your garden.

How long are your arms? What's that got to do with anything? How long your arms are determines the width of your bed. How far can you comfortably reach? I can reach 2 and half feet easily. If your arms are shorter, then make you beds narrower. This makes working in your beds much easier, after all this is the lazy person's way to garden.

Lay out your plan on the ground to see how it looks.

Plan where you will put your pipe for your watering system. This can either be above ground or buried.

Determine how wide you are going to make the pathways between the beds. I recommend about 3 feet, however, use your own judgment.

WHAT TOOLS ARE REQUIRED?

Tools are a special thing to me. I love tools. Good tools, great tools, expensive tools, cheap tools and everything in between. Most of the tools that I recommend, and tools that you need, you probably all ready own. If you must buy tools then buy the best quality that you can afford. Do not believe that only the name brand stuff is best. There are a lot of discount tool sources around. I have bought a lot of tools on eBay and Amazon. My favorite discount tool store is Harbor Freight Tools. They have a store nearby and this is unlucky for me because I buy too much. Tool List for raised bed gardening:

- Shovel round point
- Shovel square point
- Spading fork
- Long handled 3 or four tined hoe or rack
- Sledge hammer
- Portable electric drill
- Portable electric saw.
- Flat blade screw driver
- Phillips screw driver
- Slip joint pliers
- Miscellaneous drills
- Assorted garden trowels
- Garden hoe
- Wheel barrow; when it comes to wheel barrows I have a real preference to the kind with two wheels in front. They are easier to maneuver in a garden

and don't tip over so easily.

- Pruning clippers
- Claw hammer
- Some type of heavy metal bar—to make stake holes. My favorite is a piece of ¾ inch square bar from an old rod weeder.
- Hatchet This may be a small hand axe or anything that you can use to sharpen stakes and cut branches.
- Garden sprayer—hand held.
- Spray bottle
- Scissors
- Garden Rake
- Pitch fork
- Miscellaneous small garden tools. Choose what you like.

A four tine rake is one of my favorite raised bed gardening tools. It is used for bed preparation in the spring and a multitude of other tasks.

That's quite a list. You probably have most of them. Don't go out and buy a tool unless you really need it. If it's expensive and you only need it once—rent it. Tools are BSO for me (Big Shiny Objects—things that I want, don't really need and cost a lot of money.) Buy what you need. This is all about growing food and saving money.

WHAT MATERIALS ARE REQUIRED?

The intent of this book is to help you to avoid high cost to create your raised beds. If you can afford the best materials than buy them, however, there is a lot of recyclable stuff that

45

will work just as well. The materials that you will require for the construction of the bed frame and walls fall into these broad areas:

- Wall material—boards, old cement blocks, cement board, old building siding and so forth. Make sure that any wood is treated to prevent rot.
- Material for posts and stakes. This can range from old steel fence post to brand-new ornamental posts. Again make sure that any wood is treated to prevent rot.
- Miscellaneous screws and nails.
- Other hardware as needed

When you are building a lot of beds and have little money being the community collector helps. I collect old and discarded building materials to build my raised beds.

HOW TO CONSTRUCT A RAISED BED

Raised bed construction is just like any other building project. You need to have a plan. I have never drawn a formal plan for raised beds. The sequence of construction goes something like this:

Lay out your individual beds in your garden. This works unless you are like me and don't get everything done the first time. My first raised beds (see snow pictures of my garden) were not done with walls. These beds were just mounds of growing medium constructed to promote maximum plant growth. If you need to fix your beds and continue construction from year to year that is okay too.

Dig out the bottom of the beds. I like to dig out my beds two feet below the ground surface and put the dirt to the side. This is the part that takes work. I cheat as I do gardening by

CHARLES L (BUD) EVANS

John Deere. Our little 20 horse power compact tractor with a front bucket does the initial dig when there is room. This is a lot of work but well worth the effort. This first removal of the soil allows you to provide adequate drainage for the bed. It also provides an easy path for deep rooted plants.

At this point I usually put up the walls. When I use old sheet metal the metal provides a barrier for most of the deep rooted weed and plants that might penetrate the bed. We have lots of grasses here in Eastern Washington that spread by their roots. These grasses don't seem to go under the metal walls. The walls are constructed by driving stakes or posts into the ground at the edge of the beds. The metal is then fastened to the posts. My 5 foot by 5 foot bed has a post at each corner and one in the middle of each panel. The beds that are 5 feet wide and longer have posts or stakes about every four feet. If you feel that you need to put 2 X 4's to stiffen and support the sides, then use them. This depends a lot upon what kind of material you are using for the walls. Just be sure that your wall materials have high rot resistance and a long life.

After I have the walls up I fill in the bottom of the bed. Believe it or not most anything can be use in the bottom foot of the bed. Mine are filled with old limbs, discarded wood, wood chips, hay, straw, old paper bags cardboard, small and medium rocks. In general, anything that will provide drainage and trap nutrients for the bed makes good fill materials.

After the bottom is filled in, the bed is covered with a layer of cardboard, old paper sacks, old feed sacks or anything that will create a decomposable barrier over the bottom layer.

The next 6 inches or so is soil that was removed from the bed.

On top of the soil a layer of organic material is placed. This can be manure, straw, old hay, compost (if you have enough but compost is best used later), grass clippings or even wood chips.

The next layer needs to be compost or manure. You could even buy potting soil for this layer. Some of the authors that talk about small raised beds talk about this. This not an option for my bed as it just costs too much. This layer really needs to be loaded with nutrient. Since I am not an organic gardening purist, many times I will seed this layer with commercial fertilizer.

My next layer is another layer of heavy organic stuff like old hay, straw, wood chips or if I have enough compost. Rotted manure works well here also. If there is a lot of woody material in this layer it is seeded heavy with a high nitrogen fertilizer.

The top layer of the bed is composed of garden soil, the stuff you dug out and compost. By this time you should have a mound above your bed of about 6 inches to a foot. This won't last long. Put a lot of water on your bed and let it set a while. The aging of the bed is why most of my new beds are started in the fall and finished in late winter before planting begins.

If I am going to plant seeds in a raised bed a little extra preparation might be in order. Screen the top layer of soil after you have completed your bed. What I use is a frame with quarter inch hardware cloth on it. It is about 2 and half feet square. This takes out all of the bigger pieces and makes seeding small seeds easier.

See the Kindle Edition for some nice pictures of raised beds.

WATERING SYSTEMS

Everyone has his own preference for watering a garden. It doesn't seem to make much difference as to what kind of sys-

CHARLES L (BUD) EVANS

tem is used, if the garden gets the right amount of water. Here lies the secret. Different plants need different amounts of water. My rhubarb takes more water than my herbs and some dummy planted them next to one another. We are working on that problem. Think I will start a new rhubarb bed this year and dig out the old one next year, all because of a lack of planning.

There are basically three types of watering system:
- Overhead sprinklers
- Flood irrigation
- Drip systems and modified micro irrigation systems.

My favorite is drip irrigation and modified micro irrigation systems. What do I mean by modified micro irrigation systems? This is a system that might use micro sprinkler, in line drippers and perforated hose. Soaker hose also can be used with this type of system. Usually these systems operate on less than 20 pounds per squaring pressure. The real drawback to these systems is that your water needs to be quite clean. Our irrigation water, from a pressurized system, is really dirty. A sand filter will be installed this year and back flushed as necessary. This will provide clean water to our micro system. This is a lot of extra work but necessary.

Overhead sprinklers are rotating sprinklers on a riser pipe that is generally taller than you tallest plants. I like using this type of irrigation on my field corn. This is one of the simplest irrigations systems to set up. Just run pipes or a hose to each sprinkler and you are done. If you have tall risers; you may need to stake them to prevent the wind from blowing the risers over. This type of system works at line pressure whatever that may be, usually in the 45 psi to 60 psi range.

DEADLY 21ST CENTURY Copyright 2013 Benton City Consulting LLC

Flood irrigation is just that, the garden is flooded with water. This does not work too well with raised beds.

There is a lot of information on the web about drip irrigation systems. Do your research because I can't tell you what is best. Everyone's garden is different and the way that it gets water is different also. Here is a fairly good source on drip irrigation. http://www.dripirrigation.com

FENCING

Why do I include fencing in a raise bed gardening book? Well, unless you live in Whims Villa you are going to have critters running around. If you have a small farm or just some acreage, you will have critter problems. The critters I am talking about in general are the one that we raise. These can include:

Dogs
Chickens
Sheep
Cows
Deer
Rabbits

Two legged creatures with hands, sometimes we call them small children.

When you can afford it, my favorite fencing is chain link. I don't go to all the pains that are exercised for commercial chain link security fence. We just put in posts and brace posts. Then the chain link fabric is stretched up next to the posts. The fabric is rapped on the ends and stapled to the posts. My preference is 6 foot chain link because our zoning won't let us put up a higher fence without a special permit and in Benton County Washington they are a pain and expensive.

50

CHARLES L (BUD) EVANS

If you look at the pictures of my gardens you will see that most of the fence is woven wire. Here I suggest that you use less than four inch square woven wire with all the squares the same from bottom to top. Three inch squares might be better if you have a lot of chickens.

1. Building a fence is simple:
2. Just lay out the area to be fenced.
3. Mark your corners
4. String a line from corner to corner.
5. Measure the distance that you have decided to separate your post. Get this from the PLAN you made.
6. Dig post holes for the corner posts and the brace posts.
7. The other posts for the fence can either be set posts (those you dig a post hole for), or driven posts.
8. Make sure that you have planned for your gates.

Don't build your gates until you have your fence built. I don't know how it happens but my gates never fit if I build them first. That is probably why I don't buy gates. The other problem with purchased gates is that they are darn expensive. Install your gates and you are done.

A fence is a very important part of a garden if you are planning to produce a lot of food for your family. My neighbor's chickens destroyed over 500 pounds of tomatoes in my garden last year because I did not have an adequate fence.

SEEDS AND SEEDING ALSO BEDDING PLANTS

What you plant in your garden is what you get, if you are lucky. I have had a few humorous happenings from seed packages. All companies make mistakes. The one that really was funny was the cayenne pepper seed that turned out to be hot

51

thia peppers. I knew that when the peppers started to turn various color that something was wrong. They were hot. We also got some pumpkin seed that was supposed to jack o lantern sized pumpkins and they turned out to be giant pumpkins some of them near 200 pounds.

Getting the wrong seed does not happen very often but enjoy it when it does.

I generally buy my seeds at these stores:

Gurneys

Henry Fields

Burgess

Fred Meyers

Wal-Mart

Local farm stores

Amazon.com

Baker's Rare Seeds

As you can see I am not particular where I get the seeds. When it is large volume seed such as several pounds of corn seed then it is purchased locally. Some of the seeds that I use are purchased on line. You can get your seeds most anywhere. Most of the seeds I have purchased have had good germination rates.

I store emergency seeds in a sealed container in a refrigerator. These are supposed to be good for several years.

Should you buy hybrid seed or non-hybrid seed, sometimes called heirloom seeds? Many times the hybrid seed out performs the open pollinated varieties. Just remember that you can't save hybrid seed and expect to get good result from the saved seed. If you are saving seed from open pollinated varieties I recommend that you maintain adequate separation from any hybrid varieties and other varieties of the same plant, i.e. peppers.

CHARLES L (BUD) EVANS

Raised bed gardening is particularly suited to bedding plants. These are those plants that are pre-started such as tomatoes. Most vegetable varieties can be started and transplanted. There are two ways to get bedding plants. You can buy the plants at nearly any garden center in the spring. The other way is to start your own in containers in the house. My preference is to start the plants myself especially peppers and tomatoes.

If you are going to start your own bedding plants then you need to do it six to eight weeks before you plan to plant them in your beds.

It is a lot of fun going to the garden stores and looking for plants in the spring. Unless you are a lot more resistant to plants than I am, you will almost always come home with something. My problem is that usually I buy too many.

Planting small seeds in your raised beds can be challenging. Direct seeding of small seed in raised bed require that you follow seed spacing guide lines. I can't tell you what spacing for all plants but this is the general rule that I follow. Space the seeds one half the recommended distance for ordinary row gardening. The spacing should be in all directions from the seed. Place you seeds individually where you want the plant and no more than two seeds at each location. You may need to thin them as they grow.

Careful planting of small seeds means less work later on. This is one reason that I screen the last layer in my raised beds that will contain things that have small seeds like carrots.

WEEDS AND MULCH

Mulching is very important for raised bed gardens. This is your primary barrier to weeds. The bed must be weeded until the plants are large enough to put down a thick layer of mulch. I use old hay, straw, grass clipping and sometimes cardboard and paper as a mulch.

When the plants are large enough I place a layer of mulch around the plants covering the whole bed. This layer must be thick enough to shut out most of the light that shines on the soil. As you plants get larger they will provide additional shade and deter weed growth. You will need to pull any weeds that come through your mulch.

This is where intensive raised beds really begin to pay off. Your weeding time will be about one tenth of that required in a conventional garden. The raised beds bring the weeds up to your level for easy care. I am about 70 years old and raised beds eliminate a lot of bending. Building raised bed also provides me with good exercise.

SUMMARY

This guide is aimed at those that want to grow a large amount of produce in a small space. This does not mean that flowers and other plants grown for their beauty cannot be grown in raised beds. You can make your bed a work of art and still have all of the advantages of raised bed. I admit that I have a few flowers planted in some of my garden beds. Every year we plant marigold and asters in our beds. The excuse is that they help keep the bugs out. The real reason probably is that I like the color in the garden.

We provide vegetables and produce for thirteen people from our garden each year. The garden provided salads and vegetable for about 5 months fresh. We preserved 100 quarts of corn, 40 or so quarts of tomatoes, salsa, 30 some quarts of

CHARLES L (BUD) EVANS

beets and we still have carrots in the ground to be pulled and used the end of January.

WHAT ARE BEDDING PLANTS?

These are plants that you transplant into a garden in early spring to get a quicker and more reliable harvest. These plants are usually grown indoors either in a green house, under lights or in a sunny window.

The object is to start the plants 6 to 8 weeks before the last frost date. This allows the plant to have a head start on the season. Bedding plants allow for the starting and ensuring an adequate growing season for many long season plants. Many types of produce could not be grown to maturity without starting the plants indoors.

This section will lead you through starting bedding plants the easiest way possible and spending the least money. It is not meant to be an all inclusive source on starting plants. If there is an area that you don't understand do you own research? This guide will get you started growing your own plants for a small or large home garden.

WHEN TO START YOUR SEEDS.

You need to determine when to start your seeds based upon your last frost date. The best way to determine your last frost date is by experience. Our last frost date is a little later than our neighbors on the hill behind us. Our last frost date is usually about May 15th while some of our neighbors have a last frost date of about May 1st to 5th.

If you don't know your last frost date it can be obtained from the local County Extension Service in the United States. Other countries have different agencies for this information.

Just do your research as this is important. Please remember that this may not be completely accurate for your property. We are also dealing with weather and climate here so there is no exact date. It is an approximate date.

While you are determining your last spring frost date you should also determine your location's first frost date in the fall. This is important information to use in selecting the right plants. The time between the last frost date and the first frost date is the growing season for most plants.

That being said you need to start your plants 6 to 8 weeks before you plan to transplant them to your garden. Different plants will be started at different times to allow adequate growth time before transplanting. Some plants like spinach, cabbage and Swiss chard can stand light frost.

You need to start working on how you will grow your bedding plants about two weeks before the seeding date. There are a lot of things to do before you plant your seeds

PREPARING FOR YOUR SEEDLINGS

The first thing to consider is where you are going to grow your seedlings. Your seedlings need a warm well lighted place to grow. I try to find a south window that get lots of natural sunlight. In addition to sunlight I usually use additional light. This can be either daylight natural spectrum florescent light with a temperature rating of 6500 degree K or greater or the plant growing bulbs can be used. This year because of space limitations my only window is north facing. The seed trays are placed on a rack with lights installed. Because of the lack of natural light the lights will need to remain on 24 hours a day.

CHARLES L (BUD) EVANS

This guide is written from the stand point of saving money not spending it. For this reason the seedling rack is build out of scrap materials. It is 18 inches wide by 6 foot tall and four feet long. The materials came from an old crate that a neighbor gave me. The crate was disassembled for the 2 X 4's for the frame. The shelves are from an old sheet of press board that was left over from a project last year. I am not going to give you step by step instructions on how to build these racks how-ever the pictures should provide adequate information.

CONTAINERS FOR STARTING YOUR PLANTS.

You will need trays to start your plants. I like trays that are about 3 inches deep 12 to 16 inches wide and 16 to 18 inches long. This allows for a wide source of planting trays. Trays in this size range are easy to handle and provide adequate depth for the seedling to start before the first transplant. These same trays can be use for the second transplanting before the final transplant.

I did not have time to build the trays this year so I cheated. I went to the store to buy plant starting trays. Those that were available were plastic trays with peat pots in them and plastic trays with a growth medium in them. Peat pots were also available. Some of the supermarket starting kits had shallow trays with plastic covers for the seeds to retain moisture and heat. You can get really fancy with seed starting equipment. There are heat tapes available to place under your plants and other things to help get a quick start for your seeds.

After looking at the seed starting equipment that was available I decided that none of them met my needs. The cost of these set ups ranged from about $6.00 to more than $10.00

and this was just too costly for the number of plants that I wanted to start. I went to the baking pans and found disposable roaster pans that were about 3 inches deep and 13 inches by 16 inches in size. These looked good to me and they only cost about $2.50 per tray. Each tray came with a raised plastic cover, wow just what I needed to start my seeds. Then I went to the local wholesale warehouse and bought a large bag of potting soil for $10.00. This medium seems to be just about right for starting plants.

The trays were filled with potting soil, watered and allowed to set for a few days. This allows the moisture to spread throughout the planting medium. Your trays are now ready for seeds.

A good alternate way to start your bedding plants is to use medium size paper or plastic cups. Fill them with potting soil and plant a couple of seeds in each one. You can thin them later. The cup should have a couple of small holes in the bottom for drainage. I recommend setting the cups in a tray to retain water for the plants and to provide drainage without a mess. The cups should be covered with clear plastic until the seeds start.

SEEDS AND WHERE TO GET THEM

Finding garden seed is the easy part. Deciding what to grow is the hard part. I usually just grow what we eat and then try something unusual.

We have seed available at all the grocery stores in our area. The supermarkets like Wal-Mart, Fred Meyers, Target and Winco Groceries, all carry a fairly good assortment of seeds.

CHARLES L (BUD) EVANS

Most brands of seeds are okay as long as you purchase those labeled for the current growing year. I use a variety of brands. My favorites are Burpee, Henry Fields, Ed Hume and any heirloom seed producer.

As far as I am concerned there are only two types of seeds.

Heirloom

Hybrid

Heirloom seeds are those that have been around for generations and are open pollinated. I classify all open pollinated seeds as heirloom. What is open pollinated anyway? These are plants that the seed can be collected from and you can expect them to produce the same plant next year.

Hybrid plants are those that are crossed to produce specific traits. Many of these do not breed true for the succeeding generations of the plants. If you are going to save seed don't expect to save seeds from hybrid plants. The seed will probably grow but you probably will get some surprises when it comes to the fruit produced for seeds saved from hybrid plants.

GMO seeds, what are they? Genetically Modified Organisms are those that have had the DNA code modified by injecting DNA from another organism in to the DNA strands. The most common reason is to provide either greater yield or resistance to some kind of pest. I don't like getting sprayed with bug spray and I don't like insecticides in my food. My advice is to stay away from GMO seeds. Besides you can't save the seed and reuse it. These are patented seeds. If these seeds cross pollinate with your seed and you save the seed for future planting, then you are guilty of patent infringement and the seed company can sue you for damages. They have done this many times even when the pollen from their seed was wind borne for long distances.

You need to choose your own seed and plants. Go have some fun and buy your seeds. If you want to buy your seeds on line then do so.

PLANTING YOUR SEEDS AND GROWING YOUR TRANSPLANTS

Planting your seeds is the fun part. I can't wait to see how they will germinate and show their first leaves. The starting trays have been filled with potting soil or whatever mix of soil that you want to use to start your seeds. One thing to avoid is using soil that might contain weed seed. This is the reason that I buy potting soil. It is usually pretty sterile.

If you don't want to buy potting soil I would suggest that you put it in the oven at about 300 degrees for a few minutes to sterilize it. How long it needs to be heated depends upon the depth of your container. If you do this, be careful of fire and of getting burned by the hot containers. A good potting soil contains a lot of organics and some of them may burn easily.

The next step is to plant your seeds. Make a shallow cut in the potting soil and careful place your seeds in the cut. Be careful to allow enough space between the seeds. I never seem to get this right. Mine are always too close together. The most important thing to do at this step is to be sure to label what seeds you plant where. Oh, I know that you can remember but my experience is that you won't at least I don't. I use the bulk pop sickle sticks that you can get at any craft store for markers. They are easy to write on and easy to push into the soil. Many times the sticks are broken in the middle to allow the cover for the tray to go over.

60

CHARLES L (BUD) EVANS

We have tomato plants that are about a week old. I got them too close together again. The cabbage plants on the left hand side are for my grand kids' school contest to see who can grow the largest cabbage. These tomato plants will need to be transplanted into larger containers in the next day or two.

There a pictures of how to raise bedding plants in the Kindle Edition. I did not have high enough resolution pictures to include them in a print edition.

TRANSPLANTING YOUR SEEDLINGS

There are a lot of ways to transplant seedlings. What I usually do is take pop sickle stick and split it in half the long direction. This is my transplanting tool. The seedlings are carefully separated in the starting tray and the individual plants removed and transplanted into a new larger container. The trays that I moved cabbage and broccoli to are old plant containers that were saved from last year. The picture below is of the plants just after transplanting. These probably won't get a second transplant into larger pots as our outdoor temperature should be okay for them when these plants get too large for the little pony packs. (See Picture in Kindle edition.)

CONDITIONS NECESSARY TO GROW HEALTHY BEDDING PLANTS

There are a number of things to consider, to ensure that your plants start easily and stay healthy.

- The soil used should be sterile.
- The soil should be porous and be able to hold moisture easily.
- The temperature for germination should be 60 to 70 degrees F.

- Your plants, after germination, need all the light that they can get. Mine in the pictures are not getting enough light.
- You should transplant the seedling soon after germination and before the plants form a second leaf pair.
- Extreme care needs to be used during transplanting.
- Don't be afraid to try something new.

SUMMARY

Growing bedding plants is not hard. Once that you try it you won't ever be satisfied with going to the garden center and buying your plants. There will be years when it is necessary due to time available, space and other thing that get in the way of starting your own plants. Don't despair next year is another year and there is always the fall garden to get started.

The essential things for starting bedding plants are:

- Planning
- A place to start them
- Planting medium
- Light
- Water
- Good seed
- Time to care for the plants
- Desire to do it yourself
- Temperature
- Necessary materials.

Starting bedding plants is a very easy thing to do and can save quite a bit of money. Last year I spent over $250.00 on bedding plants. This year with the setup shown in this paper, my cost should be less than $150.00 for twice as many plants.

62

CHARLES L (BUD) EVANS

Starting bedding plants also allows me to start growing things a couple of months sooner and I love that. I also love giving excess plants to my neighbors.

An alternate method of starting plants is to put your potting soil in medium to large sized plastic beverage cups. Then put a couple of seeds in each one. Thin the seedlings to one plant per cup. This eliminates the need to do transplants but in the beginning it takes a lot more room.

RESOURCES FOR BEDDING PLANTS:

Your local county extension office.

Our blog Path to Self Sufficiency: We provide a lot of information that you might like on our blog.

http://pathtoselfsufficiency.budsgoldmine.com/blog/

CHAPTER 8
VEGETABLE GARDENING

PLANNING

The usual way to start any project is to define what the project is. So what is vegetable garden? Hey, this is an easy question. I'm sorry for the joke but a vegetable garden, to me, is a place where you grow food to eat. It might be several acres or a couple of containers of tomatoes on the balcony of your apartment. This is a vegetable garden.

The real key is that you grow something. Everyone can grow some of their own food. Why is it important that you grow your own food? The next few sentences may scare the daylights out of you. This country has the lowest reserves of food in its history.

If you doubt this do your research. Google is wonderful but scary. Search for such things as "US food reserves". You might want to search for something like "US grain reserves". When you do these searches you will find two groups. Those that want to scare you into thinking you will starve tomorrow and those that think the government has it all taken care of. Both of these groups are wrong. You will need to make your own choice. In any case no matter who is right you need to be prepared. You must be prepared and one part of being prepared is growing your own food and becoming as self sufficient a possible. This is what this section is all about.

So, your back and have decide to grow a garden. Let's get started. It is time to make a decision about where you are going to grow your garden. Here are a few options:

- A container garden on your door step: This is an option if you don't have a yard.
- In a multi-family public garden area.
- Till up part of your front lawn if the locals will let you.
- Till up your back yard.
- If you have a little extra acreage—then dedicate it to a garden.
- There are lots of other options to consider in finding a place to grow a garden. You have decided to grow a garden. You will find a place.

MEASURE YOUR GARDEN AREA.

I mean take a tape measure and measure the area where you will put your garden. This is a must for the following reasons:

It will help you to decide what you are going to plant.

Measurements will help to decide what kind of garden you want for example an intensive raised bed garden or a plane old flat garden.

- You measurements will help you to plan for the cost of your garden:
- Cost of materials
- Cost of seed and bedding plants.
- Cost of irrigation as needed.
- Number of hours you must spend tending your garden.
- What the return from your garden can be.

After you have measured the area where you want to put your garden you will need to make a scale drawing of it. Also do a scale drawing of the lot surrounding your garden with the

CHARLES L (BUD) EVANS

garden in it. I admit that this is one place that I have not followed my own advice. My excuse is that I have many acres that are setting idle. Just because I didn't do it doesn't mean that you don't need to create this drawing. Bite the bullet and do it.

HOW BIG SHOULD YOUR GARDEN BE?

The general rule given is this, if you are a beginning gardener, start small. I don't necessarily agree with that. My motto is to grow all of your own food that you can. The end choice on garden size is yours. You need to develop a balance between these factors:

- How much time do you have for gardening?
- How much "land" do you have for a garden?
- What are your gardening goals?
- How much will you spend on your garden and is the return worth the investment?
- What do you expect to gain from a garden personally?

If you have never gardened before and have the room a 20x 50 garden will keep you really busy. On the other hand if you have the land a 200 x 200 garden is okay, provided you have some power equipment to help out. This is another one of those choices. A relatively good garden will produce one pound or more of food per square foot.

YOUR GARDEN NOTEBOOK

This is one aspect of gardening that gets neglected. You need to keep a garden notebook or journal from day one. Look at all the information that you have collected so far and we are only a few pages into the subject.

My garden note book is a three ring binder labeled Garden Notes. I put things in this binder that are worth something to me. Do I keep as good a set of notes as I should? The answer is no. I don't have frost date or total production for any of my gardening years. I do have some rough sketches of what my garden will look like. I use these for ordering seed and preparing or buying bedding plants.

Here is a list of things that it would be helpful to have in your garden notebook:

- Last frost in the spring and first frost in the fall dates.
- What seeds you bought where.
- What produced best each year? Different plants produce better some years.
- Where you bought your bedding plants. Were they what was advertised or what they were labeled? We have had some interesting result from bedding plants.
- What pest bothered your garden and what you did to control them?
- What kind of fertilizer you used and when.
- Any information about what works for you and what doesn't.
- Any information you want to pass on to your children.

Many people make their garden note book a simple journal of their summer lives. Keep this notebook. It will pay for the effort in many unexpected ways.

I recommend that you create a sketch of your garden to scale to get the lay out right.

68

Gardening is not an exact science. Contrary to what the Extension Service says, there are no master gardeners, only some gardeners that work harder and study more than others. Anyone that grows a successful garden is a master gardener in my book. (And this is my Book.). Any garden that produces some food or a few flowers is a successful garden. Don't get discouraged if your first results aren't as good as your neighbors.

WHAT SHOULD YOUR GARDEN BE?

It is now decision time. You have most of the information that you need to plan your garden. It is time to decide what kind of garden you want:

- Just a flower garden.
- A garden that produces a few great tasting vegetables for dinner.
- A garden that produces most of the produce for your family during the summer.
- A garden that is all of the above and produces surplus food to be stored by canning, freezing or winter storage.

For myself I always choose the last option. We have lots of room and love fresh vegetables. Our crops range from spinach in the spring to potatoes for winter storage.

As mentioned before there are basically two types of gardens. These are intensive bed gardens and field or flat gardens. These two types of garden can take many forms.

An intensive bed garden can be intensive raised beds with a wall around them to hold the soil. An intensive bed garden can be a mound of soil that has been prepared to enhance plant growth. Raise intensive beds are my favorite type of garden. What are some reasons for raised intensive beds?

69

- Their production is incredible. We had a 5 foot by 5 foot bed of beets a couple of years ago that produced beets for the family throughout the summer and we canned 38 quarts by fall.
- After the beds are constructed most of the gardening work is done. Besides a bed that is 2 feet above the ground is a lot easier to weed. My beds are designed so that I can reach the center of the bed from either side without too much stretching.
- Preparation for planting of an established bed is simple.

Here are the only disadvantages that I can find for raised intensive beds:

- They take a lot of work to construct. I spend at least 20 hours to construct a 5 foot by 5 foot two foot high raised bed with a wall around it. A lot of this construction is hard work.
- They cost more to prepare initially than a flat bed or mounded bed.

I recommend ordinary field gardening for crops like corn and potatoes and with potatoes there are a lot of things that must be done.

The field garden is just that. The ground is plowed up or tilled and then smoothed. I like to add manure and fertilizer at this point. Then I till it again. The steps for a field garden are these:

- Lay it out.
- Till or plow the garden.
- Rake or smooth it.
- Fertilize it.

70

- Till it again.
- Rake and smooth it to prepare a surface layer for planting.
- Plant your garden.
- Maintain the garden until it is harvested.
- Love it.

A derivative of the field method is sometimes called the French Intensive method. This method adds an additional step. It is called double digging and is just what it means. The area to be planted is dug down at least a foot to two feet. The soil is removed and then replaced as the digging proceeds. I like to add a lot of organic material at this time to loosen up the soil. This is the best method to make a garden for heavy clay soil. This method really teaches you the meaning of the word intense. It is a lot of work to create a garden using this method. I have to confess that I use this method a lot but here I garden by John Deere. My tractor does most of the work.

Given the right conditions, all of these methods will produce a respectable garden. Being lazy I don't mind working hard once and harvesting the results for a number of years. That is the reason that I am slowly converting my garden to raised bed with walls around them.

WHAT TO GROW?

How do you know what to grow? These are the things that I ask myself about what to grow in my garden:

- What does my family like to eat, if nobody is going to eat it why grow it?
- What will my climate allow me to grow?
- What will my garden support? This becomes a question of size and available plant resources.

71

- Have I checked the time required to grow each item from planting to harvest.
- If I grow too much can it be stored or given away? Try giving away zucchini squash around here in the summer.

These are the criteria that I use to select my garden plants.

Your climate is a definition of your growing season. The best source of information is the USDA Plant Hardiness Zone Map. The web site for this map is http://planthardiness.ars.usda.gov/PHZMWeb/. This is a really nifty site please check this one out.

After you determine your zone it is easy to find the average last frost date and first fall frost date. Here is a nice site for length of growing season. http://www.basic-info-4-organic-fertilizers.com/hardinessmap.html I don't even have an affiliate link to them. After I have determined the hardiness zone and the length of the growing season it is time to proceed to the seed catalogs. Here you will need to look at each plant you plan to grow to determine if it will grow in your climate. This book can't do that for you. We live in the Mecca of gardening. Our hardiness zone is 7a on the 2012 map and our growing season is usually from about May 15 to about October 15th. You must do your own research. I say it again you must do your own research for the location of your garden.

WHAT ARE MY FAVORITE THINGS TO GROW?
Here is a list of my favorite vegetables:
Peppers
Corn
Potatoes
Tomatoes
Peas

CHARLES L (BUD) EVANS

Beets
Lettuce
Kohlrabi
Parsnips
Carrots
Radishes
Cabbage
Broccoli
Brussels sprouts, (This is one vegetable that I have not been very successful at growing.)
Rhubarb
Turnips
Spinach
Chard
Various Squash
Pumpkins

If I have missed anything that you want grow, please feel free to add it. I realize the rhubarb might not be classified as a vegetable; however, it grows like a vegetable.

This should get you started with your garden planning. There are three P's of a successful garden:

Prayer
Planning
Persistence

TOOLS

Any project requires tools for its completion. Gardening is no different. There are a few specific tools that you need. There are a lot of tools that are available that may not be needed. I like tools; therefore, I spend too much on tools. The following tool list is similar but different to the one listed in raised bed gardening. This one is aimed at flat gardening instead of raised bed gardening.

Buying tools is necessary and there are a few things to keep in mind before you purchase a tool. Always buy the best quality tool you can afford. Price is an indicator of quality; however, the highest price tool is not always the best quality. You will need to judge the quality of tools that you purchase.

Buying used tools is an option. There are yard sales, second hand stores and various internet sites that sell used tools. One of my friends has obtained nearly all of his tools at yard sales and they are top quality tools.

If you are only going to use a tool once or twice it might be better to rent the tool instead of purchasing it.

Here is a list of what I consider the needed tools. Yes this is duplicated in the section on raised bed gardening, but you will notice if you read closely that there are some significant differences. Buy power tools only if you need them as they are expensive and require quite a bit of maintenance:

Hand Tools
Round pointed shovel
Spading fork
Bow rake
Garden hoe
Small hand hoe
Various trowels and planting tools
Stirrup hoe
Pitch fork
4 tine rake/cultivator
Clippers/pruning equipment
Heavy scissors
Small stirrup hoe

CHARLES L (BUD) EVANS

Hammer, screw drivers, pliers

Post bar, any kind of heavy steel bar for starting driven posts and digging post holes.

Hand post hole digger, only if you have a lot of fencing to do.

Gloves

Wheel Barrow

Power tools—only buy those that you really need.

Lawn Mower

String trimmer

Mini-tiller

Garden tiller

Lawn and Garden Tractor

Compact tractor

Chipper/shredder

Buy or obtain a good quality wheel barrow. My favorite is the model with two wheels in front. The two wheeled wheel barrow has better stability and will carry a larger load with less effort. The single wheel model is more maneuverable in a garden.

TOOL MAINTENANCE

Garden tool maintenance and storage is a do as I say not as I do issue. Frankly I don't maintain and care for my garden tools as well as I should. Your tools need to be stored in a shelter out of the weather and sun. So please do as I say and not as I do (No one is perfect, right.).

Wooden handled tools need to have their handles maintained. The original finish on garden tools handles is not usually very durable. The best finish for wooden handles is the old linseed oil finish. This is applied by lightly sanding the old finish off the handle and then applying several coats of linseed oil. This is not the only finish to use but it works. You can visit your local home improvement center for other options.

Keep your tools sharp. This not only makes you tool safer but it reduces the amount of effort needed use the tool.

Good tools should last a life time with proper care. Many tools are passed down from parent to child.

POWER TOOLS

There are two power tools that you will want to have for a garden and the good thing is that if you have a lawn and a yard you already have these two. You will need a lawn mower and a string trimmer.

Buy a lawn mower that is appropriate for the yard that you have. If you have a small to medium size yard a push mower with a rear grass catcher is adequate. Personally I cannot see a lot of difference in these mowers so almost any will do.

For a string trimmer my opinion is to buy the best that you can afford. I like those that use a detachable power head. This allows you to buy various attachments' such as a mini-tiller. If you do raised bed gardening, a mini-tiller can be very helpful. If you have a fairly large row garden, then a mini-tiller is almost a must have tool.

If you have a fairly large row or field garden then a roto-tiller is probably necessary. At least it is necessary in the beginning. If you setup you garden using one of the methods that require less tillage, you may not need to own a roto-tiller. Consider renting a tiller when you need it. Maybe you can borrow one from a neighbor.

Buy a lawn and garden tractor only if you really need it. They are expensive and this is all about producing food and

CHARLES L (BUD) EVANS

saving money. If you buy a lawn and garden tractor try to get a model that has attachments available for various tasks.

Compact tractors are necessary only if you have a lot of ground and need to maintain it. My compact tractor is a John Deere 755 with a loader. I got mine in a pile of parts and rebuilt it about 10 years ago. This tractor. to buy it today, would cost about $10,000 on the used market. If you need a tractor, shop around.

This chapter is not meant to be a comprehensive guide to tools but as a place to start. Do your own research and reading to find those that are best suited to you.

SOIL AND GROUND PREPARATION

The life blood of a garden is the soil. The soil provides nutrients for the plants and holds the water that the plant needs to pick up the nutrients and move the nutrient up the plant stem. The root system of the plant is the supplier of the solid material that a plant requires. Your soil determines what you plant root system will be like. You need to provide the best possible place for your plant roots.

FIELD GARDENS

Field gardens are those that are fairly large in area and are usually used for such crops as potatoes and corn. Many people plant their whole garden this way. The garden is laid out like a farmer's field and tilled to prepare the seed bed. The plants are planted in rows with a space between for growth and a path for maintaining the rows. This is the conventional method of gardening. This method is fairly labor intensive as these patches require yearly tilling and a lot of weeding.

You can combine one of the intensive gardening methods with field gardens. This will reduce your labor and increase your yields. You won't see a great decrease in labor the first year but the second year, if you apply mulch generously the first year and the second year the amount of weeding needed should decrease.

How do you start a new field garden? I like to start a new garden the fall before it is to be planted. These steps to put a garden in order for spring planting are somewhat like these, there probably is no one method better than another, so just do what feels right.

First you need to clear and cleanup your garden patch. Remove all of the weeds and mow the area.

Till the area two or three times. I usually till it first by going around the garden. Then I till it from corner to corner from two directions.

Let it set a while.

Rake out the roots and other stuff. This goes into the compost pile.

Till it again. These few steps should be completed before the first snow or when the ground freezes.

Early in the spring cover your new garden with manure or compost.

Till in the compost and manure.

You can raise a good garden without compost and manure by using commercial fertilizers, however, these never seem quite as good as using natural materials. Even with natural materials it may be necessary to provide additional plant food by using commercial fertilizer.

Rake you garden to get as even a seed bed as possible.

You should now be ready to plant. If it sets for a while and weeds start then till it or rake it to remove the weeds.

CHARLES L (BUD) EVANS

A variation to the conventional garden us a layered garden. I have used these with great success. These are the basic steps to build a layered garden.

Locate where you want your garden rows.

Cover the area that will be planted with cardboard old newspaper old paper sack completely. Be sure that you have a couple of layers at least.

Strip the sod from the areas between the rows and throw it on the paper layer.

Put a layer of organic material on the sod. This can be compost, manure, old grass clipping, old hay, and so forth.

The next lay is a layer of soil. I usually get it by digging between the rows. Put several inches of soil over the organic layer.

My last layer is a layer of compost or aged manure and this layer is mixed with more soil.

This layer is the planting layer.

After the plants have started and the first weeding is done you should mulch this type of garden. The mulch can be old hay, grass clipping or if you are really short of material buy a couple of bales of peat moss at the garden center.

Next year you just add a layer of compost, pull back the mulch where you want to plant and plant your garden. In a couple of years the soil will decompose and you will have a fine garden bed.

In summary soil and ground preparation is fairly simple:

Dig it up.

Fertilize it.

Rake it.

Plant it.

Oh yes, enjoy your garden. This is the most important step. If you don't enjoy a garden you won't take care of it and your plants will know it. Tell them that they are doing well and they will.

Now, here are a few words about compost.

There a volumes of material written about compost. So what is compost? The common definition of compost is that it is decomposed organic material called humus. Really that is just what compost is decomposed biological junk. It might be old leaves, hay, straw, kitchen waste, animal waste, manure or just about any biological material. In short good compost is a light brown material that smells like good fresh earth. It does not smell like the smelly waste it came from.

How do you make compost? Compost is created by mixing various organic materials together and letting them decompose. The decomposition is carried out by small microscopic animals and by bacteria. The science of decomposition is a whole life time in itself. You make compost by putting all this stuff together and letting it cook. Good compost reaches a fairly high temperature, in fact, if certain conditions exist composting or decomposition can cause a fire in the compost pile. This is most widely known as spontaneous combustion. If hay is too green and not allowed to dry properly before processing or stacking it can spontaneously combust. Compost is formed by the same process.

There are two types of decomposition of organic materials. These are:

Anaerobic, which is the decomposition without air. This is the one that is stinky and messy like sewage. In some instances this is a very valuable process for the decomposition of organics. A methane generator or bio-digester uses this process to produce methane gas for fuel.

The other process is aerobic digestion. This is the process that is generally favored for the creation of compost. It is a

80

controlled decomposition in a pile, bin, or tumbler. The secrets of aerobic digestion are the carbon to nitrogen ratio, the moisture content and the size of the particles of organic matter.

This may sound like an exact science but it isn't. Generally you just place all of your old grass clipping, kitchen waste—organic and your weeds in a pile. Add some soil to get things started and wait. Many methods exist to speed up the composting process but in my opinion they are not necessary. To avoid problems I use two compost piles. One that I use in the garden this year and one that I add waste to this year for next year. Next year I have great compost with not too much effort. The only labor is to turn the compost pile a few times during the year to ensure aerobic decomposition.

That is the story of composting.

FERTILIZERS AND SOIL PH

This is not a book about organic gardening. Organic gardening is great once that you have an established garden, lots of compost and other organic material. This is usually not the case for starting a garden. (I never have enough compost even though I make it by the ton.) At some point you are going to need to add commercial fertilizer. If you do add fertilizer do it the right way. The first question is what do you need to add? This depends somewhat upon the plants that you are going to grow in your garden.

Many berry plants like an acid soil. The acid or base content of the soil is measured by PH this is a log scale of the hydrogen ion ranging from 0 to 14. PH of 7 is considered neutral. Many garden plants like a soil that is slightly acid with a ph of 6.5 to 6.9 do your research. You will need to do your research for the specific ph that your plants require. In general a slightly acid soil allows the plants to absorb the nutrients from the soil easier.

The best way to find out what your soil requires is to have it tested. Your County Extension Office can tell you how to do this and where to send the soil sample. Another way is to buy an inexpensive soil test kit at the garden center.

I have an instrument that I poke in the soil to measure the ph. This is not the most accurate method but it is good enough. Generally my soil is tested with a store bought test kit. These are not the most accurate but are good enough for growing a great garden.

My one challenge for ph has been blue berries. Our soil is quite alkaline from years of irrigation and high nitrogen fertilizer. In addition about ten years ago our farm was burned over by a very high temperature ground fire. This removed most of the organics from the soil. This has created a real challenge to return the soil to a productive state. One successful method to rebuild the soil is building raised beds.

Your soil PH can be adjusted by adding sulfur to alkaline soil or lime to acid soil. Be careful when you do this. This is one time to really do a good job of researching what you need and asking around the neighborhood. The really great thing about gardening as we have described it is that you won't have these problems after your garden is established. The exceptions are those plants that require a quite acid soil or a very alkaline one. These types of plants will require special care for soil preparation.

CHARLES L (BUD) EVANS

CHAPTER 9
MAINTAIN GOOD HEALTH: STORE NEEDED MEDICATIONS.

Many of us have medical needs that might not be available at the local pharmacy in an emergency. I recommend that you keep at least a three months supply of medications such as heart medication, blood pressure medication and all diabetic supplies and Insulin. Some types of insulin can be stored up to a year in the refrigerator. You can rotate your medications to ensure that you always have a fresh supply. You will need to discuss emergency preparedness for your medications with your doctor.

There are many natural and herbal medicines that are useful to maintain in your emergency supplies.

Many people stay healthy by living a healthy life style. Eat right, particularly fruits and vegetables that can be home grown and stored at home. One of the greatest advantages of home canned food is that you know what's in it.

If you have a medical condition that needs treatment, it can be a good idea to do some research and see if there is a natural remedy for the situation. As always discuss the use of these substances with your doctor.

Adequate exercise is a good step toward a healthy life style. I have always thought that a couple of hours of hard work in the garden should be just as good as going to the gym and a lot more productive. Gardens are a part of a healthy life style from many perspectives.

I will not attempt to tell you how to meet your medical needs. My advice is to do your research and talk with competent medical personnel. Some doctors will work with you to use natural remedies. Not all doctors fall under the AMA and pharmaceutical companies' methodology. Treat the symptom with a drug and not look for a cure at the source. This philosophy has lead to our current problem with antibiotic resistant bacteria and virus.

CHAPTER 10
MAINTAIN A POSITIVE AND CHEER-FUL ATTITUDE

Most of the things that we worry about are beyond our control. If you can't change it why worry about it. How you feel about everything is really under the control of your mind. We can choose how we will react to a situation. An example of this happened to me. I was in Walmart with my Batman cap on. It is a low key black cap. A man came up to me and asks how I could possibly wear that hat after the shootings that had taken place by a man wearing a Batman hat. I could have responded that I didn't care or any other response but I choose to just smile and walk away. The bottom line is that my cap is not a symbol of someone that is going to shoot up a crowd of people. Yes I am sorry that that disaster happened, however, I can't do anything about it. I was not there to stop the shooter.

This is a perfect example of something that is beyond your control and there is nothing that you can do about it. My question is, why worry about it? There are three points in time that are important in our lives. These are the past, the present, and the future. The past is good for lessons learned. We can't change it but we can learn from the past. Why should we worry about the past as we cannot change one jot or line or one whit of it.

The present is what we need to be concerned about. This exact instant is the only place in time that we can change anything. I view it like this. I draw two lines in the dirt and step between the lines. This represents the present. Behind me is the past and in front of me is the future. The present is where we can make a difference. Your actions should be based upon what you want the future to be. Correct choices will determine the future that you want.

Okay, what can I do to change the future? In an earlier section we talked about planning and goal setting. The planning to achieve them and goals that you wish to achieve will help you to make the decisions in the present to get you the results you want in the future. A perfect example is getting out of debt. You made the decisions and choices in the past that got you into debt. There is nothing that you can do about that except learn the lesson to avoid all debt if possible. You have set a goal to get out of debt. What does that mean? That means that you will do what it takes to get out of debt. The choices to do that are made in the present.

Let's consider an example.

The phone rings, "Hi Mr. Miller, I am Sonia from miracle mile travel. You have just won a trip to the Bahamas for two. This includes free transportation and lodging."

You say, "Sure send me the tickets."

This is where the problem begins. You really want to take your significant other to the islands. The problem is that you have no cash, but you have a couple of credit cards with a lot of available credit. You think this is a chance of a life time. The fine print says that you will need to pay for your own meals during your stay. That could be several thousand dollars in expenses. You really want to take this trip. Then a nagging little voice says "What was that goal? Was it to get out of debt?"

A sudden realization hits you. I don't need to take this trip and it does not fit in with my goals. A quick calculation shows that by not going on this trip you could pay off one credit card by the end of the year. The amount that you save in interest will buy the rings that your significant other wants before the

CHARLES L (BUD) EVANS

wedding next year. The kicker is that you find that you can sell the tickets for enough to buy the ring set for your intended. Things don't always happen like this but if you have your goals and plans in place the chance of a miracle happening are a lot greater.

Now reader you are about to ask what has this got to do with feeling good and maintaining a positive attitude. Everything, you made a decision that you could control and moved toward a goal that is important. It is a lot easier to be positive and cheerful when you are on the path to your goals.

Why should you maintain a positive attitude and be cheerful? Here are a few reasons.

- It is good for your health.
- It attracts opportunity.
- You day goes faster and there is less stress.
- Many of the seemingly complex things become simple.
- How can you maintain a positive attitude when everything is going wrong?
- Live in the present.
- Take things one day at a time.
- If one day is too long, how about an hour at a time?
- Break big things down to little parts and actions.
- Change what you can and leave the rest.
- Take action that you have defined.

One of the greatest complements ever given to me was given to me at my 70th Birthday Party. A very good friend said, "No matter what kind of a lemon the world throws at him, he will turn it into lemonade or maybe even a lemon pie."

This means that you can always turn a bad situation around and use it to your advantage. It may not be what you originally wanted but it is always better than the alternative of doing nothing.

You can choose how you feel about a situation. You can choose to be depressed and down or you can choose to be upbeat with a, "I can change this attitude."

CHARLES L (BUD) EVANS

CHAPTER 11
DEVELOP GOOD COMMUNITY RELA-TIONSHIPS

What are community relations? The simplest definition is how do you get along with your neighbors. Do the people in your neighborhood help one another on a regular basis? The relationships that you want to build are neighbor helping neighbor. The best example that I can remember happened right across the road from my shop.

One afternoon a really drunk driver spun around in the intersection and took out about 100 feet of the neighbors goat pen fence. Many of the neighbors were coming home from work and most stopped to help. This is a short story because by the time that the police had the driver securely in the backseat of the patrol car the neighbors had fixed the fence to keep the neighbor's goats in their pen and off the road. One fellow went home and got a couple of posts, another got some wire and they borrowed tools from me. We all built a new fence. That fence stands today at least five years later. I live in a great neighborhood. This is the kind of relationship that we need to survive in today's environment.

How do you develop this kind of a neighborhood? I like to think of community relations as an action verb. These relationships are built by doing. You go visit your neighbor across the fence. If someone needs help you volunteer before being asked. If your neighbor is going to be gone for a while you keep an "eye" on his place. When you start doing these things then others see how nice that was and will do the same thing for someone else. After this action gets started it takes on a mind of its own and the whole neighborhood changes. People become more tolerant of one another and shortly are sharing tools and garden stuff with one another.

Good relationships with neighbors is a two way street. If you borrow something, then you return it in as good or better condition than when you borrowed it. If you break it you fix it or get the owner a new thing.

When times get rough this is one of the fundamental items necessary for survival. Just do it.

CHARLES L (BUD) EVANS

CHAPTER 12
INVENTORY YOUR SKILLS

Why do you need to know what your skills are? Good question. What are your skills? Can you list them right now and not miss half of them? Did I get your attention with all these questions? If not then close this book now and sell it to someone that will use it. Some time ago I started an inventory of what I could do well. That was okay but sometimes it's not what we can do well that counts but rather what we can do to get the job done. Perfection is not usually an option when we really need a skill and there is no one else around or we are broke and can't afford to hire a professional.

Okay, "What's so hard about a skill list, I know what I can do?" Do You? Here is my suggestion. Go back to the earlier chapter that discusses mindmapping. Make a mindmap of your skills. Then do another mindmap of the skills that you think you need. Now you're getting somewhere. Do a third mindmap of of what skills you need to upgrade. Take these three mind map and make some lists. List your best skills from most skilled at the top to least skilled at the bottom. Take your list of skills you think you might need and place those most necessary at the top and list them is descending order of importance. Take the third list of skills that need to be upgraded and list them in a decreasing order of importance. These three mindmaps and three lists will give you a picture of what skills you have and what skills you need to develop. Everyone's list will be different as we all live under different conditions and we live different lives.

Now take these lists and take action and have fun getting better at doing what you love.

Here is a list of skills that I need to Improve:

- Financial Management
- Human Reations
  - Irrigation District
  - Food Coop
- Electronics and Computer programing
- Marketing
- Medical, first aid skills

These lists can be done as Mind Maps. Freemind.com is a source of free mindmaping software. Mindmaps are a way to clear thinking. If you want to make them beautiful and have the time and talent then do it.

I originally included a list of my skills here but it appears too much like bragging. You can, however, view this list as a mindmap in the Kindle edition.

CHARLES L (BUD) EVANS

CHAPTER 13
STORING ENERGY

This could be the toughest thing to get done in the whole survival check list. Storing energy in any form can be difficult. The simplest way to store energy for heating and cooking is to have a wood burning kitchen range. When I was growing up in the mountains of Montana that is what we used. We also had a sawmill so the supply of wood was endless. Now day's things are different. I live in the desert of eastern Washington and the only wood comes from the pruning of orchards or is hauled in. Even here an old wood stove is not a bad idea.

Another way to store energy for heating and cooking is to store propane. This works fairly well. If you get a fairly large propane tank you can definitely store enough energy for cooking. We have a large propane camp stove and several propane tanks in the 7 gallon range. I do not recommend storing propane inside a building unless you have it prepared for ventilation.

A pellet stove with battery backup and an inverter will provide reliable heat for your home. Just be sure that you have a way to recharge the battery. Generally if you are in a position to store energy to heat your home you will have an auxiliary generator for electrical power. The generator can be used to charge your batteries when it is running.

A generator is a great thing to have. It will keep your freezer cold for a long time with not to much fuel. That brings up another question. How much fuel should I store for the generator? The recommended amount would be enough to provide for your needs for a year, however, that isn't to practical in all cases. My personal plan is to develop a multi fueled alternate energy system. This system will use high temperature pyrolysis to create generator fuel, solar power, wind power and two other sources of fuel oil or gas. You will need to solve this one for yourself.

CHAPTER 14
DOMESTIC ANIMAL FEED

If you have livestock then you need to store food for them. You dogs and cats probably can get by on table scraps if worst comes to worst. If you have farm animals then you will need to store food for them. We solved that problem for our chickens by raising a little over an acre of corn. Here is a link to the book I wrote called the Lord's Corn Patch. (This Book has been included in this system.) It is a Kindle book. http://amzn.to/VZbKRY If you have land then you can raise most of your animal feed. A word from a wise old man, **Don't wait until you need it to start raising your feed.** Animal feed is one area that cooperation among neighbors is really necessary. One may grow more hay than he needs and his neighbor may grow excess grain. A trade is in order to meet the needs of both.

CHAPTER 15
GET LAND TO LIVE ON AND GROW YOUR OWN FOOD.

It goes without saying that if you have read this far in this book then you want to be out of the city if you aren't already. You will need five to ten acres of land with adequate water to grow food for your family and your animals. This is not an easy undertaking. It takes work. It is worth the effort for several reasons. You know what is in your food. If there is a truckers strike your next day's meal is secure. I can't tell you how to get land. If you want this life style than set the goal and develop a plan. My best advice is to your own research. We have 20 acres as a family home stead. Two of my children and their families live here with Ma and Pa. It is also a great way to raise kids. Children live in the city, kids live on the farm.

This section is a revision of the first issue of this book. Since I wrote the original book I have been convinced that life in the city is going to get very hard almost immediately. It is February of 2013 and this country is facing massive unemployment. In my family there are four men unemployed with good skills. Two of them are college graduates. The government is printing money like they were about to run out of paper. We all know what this will lead to. This leads to hyper inflation. Now this might have some benefit to those that owe money and have a source of income that will inflate along with the cost of living. What this means is that it will take a wheel barrow full of money to buy a small bag of groceries. If you don't believe this then look at hamburger that is over $3.00 a pound when a year ago it was less than $1.50 a pound. Gasoline was about $2.00 a gallon a year or so ago. It is now almost $3.50 per gallon. The really interesting thing is that the government does not take these types of items into the calculations for inflation.

If there is any way possible you need to get a couple of acres of land. By using the right intensive gardening techniques you can grow most of your own food.

With the current real estate market your land may be the best investment that you will ever make. Current long term interest rates in 2013 are less than 5%. It won't all ways be this way but land is a good investment and they ain't going to make any more of it.

CHARLES L (BUD) EVANS

CHAPTER 16
DEVELOP STRONG SPIRITUAL BELIEFS

Your spiritual strength is what keeps you going when all the rocks are falling on you and no end is in sight. Your spiritual strength will give you the faith to keep going against all odds and succeeding. Now I won't tell you how to do this but I will share my approach with you. I am a member of the Church of Jesus Christ of Latterday Saints. The power of God gives me the strength that I need to conquer any obstacle. I have had many experiences that have given me a sure knowledge that this power does exist and will aid us if we will just ask.

I will give you a very simple but important miracle that happened just the other day in my life. I lost my keys to everything on the place but our cars. I checked all of the pockets of the clothes that I was wearing looked on the ground and in the pickup. Tore up my bed room looking, made a mess in my office and the shop looking for these keys. My daughter said, "Dad you always tell us to pray when we have a problem that we can't solve alone. Why don't you ask Heavenly Father for help? I am sure that he will help."

I was convinced that I had lost those keys at Wal-Mart. In fact my wife and I were getting ready to go to the store to check at the lost and found. Just before we were going to leave, I checked the pockets of the pants I was wearing. In the back pocket under a pair of gloves were my keys. Now I know that they were not there before because I had checked that pocket. In any case that was a prayer answered.

It is the faith and spiritual strength that keeps you going when all the chips are down. There is a saying that there are no true atheists in fox holes and I believe it.

The following book is included unedited, please take the good from it and use it.

CHARLES L (BUD) EVANS

CHAPTER 17
THE LORD'S CORN PATCH
DEVELOP STRONG SPIRITUAL BELIEFS

INTRODUCTION

This book is not one of my traditional books. It reflects my religious preferences and a decidedly Christian outlook. Again I ask you to use the grocery store method. **If you can use the information or it is entertaining to you take it with you. Don't condemn the whole book just because you disagree with one idea.** This project started with a revelation form the Lord and continues today as he has his hand upon it. My perspective is from the Church of Jesus Christ of Latterday Saints. This book is about a modern day miracle.

I can testify to you personally about most of the happenings in this book. Those that I did not personally experience will be so noted. I am a member of the Church of Jesus Christ of Latterday Saints commonly known as the Mormons. We believe in personal revelation and answers to personal prayers. This book is a testimony that these things do happen today, yesterday and they will happen tomorrow

INSPIRATION

In the middle of May 2012 I was walking around my vacant and weed ridden field near Benton City, Washington wondering what I should do with the property. We had a real dilemma on our hands as the Benton Irrigation District was assessing us over $250 per acre for the new pressurized water system. The cost of this irrigation water whether we wanted it or not was added on to our taxes. The challenge was what to do to pay the cost of the water and how could we make it pay its own way?

A small voice came into my mind saying, "Why don't you plant some corn?" My response was immediate, "I don't have the equipment, seed and besides that is a lot of work". This problem continued to plight me as the days wore on. About the first of June that little voice was back again saying, "You could plant corn." My answer was the same and I ignored those promptings. About the middle of June that voice got a little more pervasive and said, "When are you going to plant your corn?" At this time I remembered a story that a friend of mine had told me.

He was from Salt Lake and had decided not to serve a mission for the Church. They were at a family outing and his uncle put his arm around him and said, "When are you going on a mission?" He thought no more about it as he was not going to serve a mission. Later that summer they were at a family outing on a lake in the area and his uncle again asked him when he was going on a mission. He blew this suggestion off again. A short time later at another family gathering his uncle asked, "When will we see your mission papers? " This time he got the message and turned in his mission application. He by his own witness stated that he had a very successful mission. When he returned from his mission he went to Uncle Tom's office in the Church Office Building to tell his Uncle about his mission. His Uncle listened with great interest and when this you man finished he said, "Don't make the Lord ask you three times again

102

CHARLES L (BUD) EVANS

to do his work." I had heard from the Lord three times to plant corn. It was time for action no matter what the cost.

PLANTING CORN

That afternoon I was out on my little John Deere tractor with a spring tooth harrow breaking up that field to plant corn. I tore up just a little over an acre. At this time our finances were in the toilet. I did not have money to buy seed, pipe for the irrigation, or even a way to get the fertilizer that had been given to me on to the corn. This was when the miracles started to happen.

I have a neighbor that is the manager of a fertilizer and seed business. I told him that I needed corn seed. He said, "Well I have some seed that we can't sell as it is 103 day to harvest corn seed and for most farms it is to late in the year to plant it. We can't hold it over to next year. I can bring up a sack of that seed for you." I got that sack of seed and it was premium hybrid corn seed. It would have cost me a couple of hundred dollars to buy seed and the Lord provided it. Now I had this ground torn up and the weeds pulled off and piled up. Another friend and neighbor asked what we were doing and I told him I was going to plant corn. He said, "You can borrow my tractor and big disk to finish plowing the ground. That is just what I did. I borrowed his tractor and disk. Of course the disk broke while I was using it but Bud is known as the master tinker and fixed the disk much better than it was before it broke. My neighbors comment was, "You did a really good job fixing my disk, what do I owe you." My answer was, "Nothing." The way things worked where I grew up was that if you borrowed something you returned it as good or better condition than when you got it. This shocked my neighbor and he said, "Boy I wish everyone felt that way." Then he proceeded to tell me of all the stuff that people had borrowed and returned broken. I am really glad that I did my best to fix that disk better than it was before. That was miracle number two.

After the ground was disked it was harrowed again with the old spring tooth harrow and I had gotten all of the rubble left from the disking removed it was time to seed. We do not have a seeder to use to seed corn with the tractor, but I knew that the corn had to be seeded. Here was my solution. I made straight rows running north and south across the ground. This provided a furrow to use to plant the corn. Please realize that an acre of corn hand planted with rows about 38 inches apart is a lot of seed to plant.

A neighbor had loaned me a Earthway Garden Seeder to use on my garden this year. It has a seed metering disk for corn. I set that seeder up and planted the corn. That seeder is a great tool and I will add one to my gardening tools for next year.

(The original document had a picture here of the Gardenway Seeder.)

You can see from this picture that it is a lot of work to seed an acre in this manner. It took me over a day to seed this ground pushing this seeder across the patch. This was another miracle that the Lord made available to me.

IRRIGATION OF THE CORN

Corn is a sub topical plant that originated on the American continent. Our current corn is a descendent of the plant called maze that the ancient Aztec grew. It requires lots of warm weather and lots of water as well as rich soil. We have planted the corn and it is about July 1st. The corn requires about 107 days to maturity for this hybrid. This means that the corn will be mature about the 15th of October if all goes well. The current problem is that it does not have any water.

104

CHARLES L (BUD) EVANS

Somehow we managed to come up with enough cash to buy the sprinkler heads and riser pipes but no money to buy the irrigation lines. I have an old pile of pvc pipe that probably is not good. My buckets of pipe fittings are always an assortment of many different pipe fittings and will provide what we need. As I go to this old pipe pile, what I need is always there. My irrigation plumbing may not be the prettiest but it works. I have named this the magic pipe pile. It supplied what I needed. When the job was complete there was little pipe left in the pile. This pile of pipe supplied more than I ever put in it. This was one of the Lord's miracles to get this corn planted.

It is into the month of July and I don't have water on the corn. If it is going to produce a crop that seed needs water now. As I am working on the irrigation lines one afternoon I look to the sky and say Lord this corn really needs water if it is to grow this year. Then I go back to work.

Either the next day or two days later, I don't remember the exact day and I did not write it my journal an unusual event occurs. We are blessed with an unprecedented summer cloud burst over the Tri-City area. This just does not happen here. This rain thoroughly soaked the corn patch. I expected help from the Lord but I did not expect him to dump a bucket of water on my corn patch. By the time that the ground was dry again I had the water system operating. The irony of this system is that I started out with 5 foot risers and by August I had to add another foot to the risers as the corn was over 8 feet tall.

The only problem with the irrigation now is that Benton Irrigation District is assessing us over $4000.00 for the water for 14.3 acres next year. That is more than the taxes; perhaps the Lord can fix this situation too.

IRRIGATION. FERTILIZER AND WEED SPRAY

In our area weeds are a real problem. We have high winds occasionally and the horse breeders haul in hay from all over the United States and it is not weed free. For these reasons we have an abundance of non-native weeds and hard to control weeds here.

I asked around about weed spray for the corn but did not come up with a good spray. Many folks suggested using 2-4-D which is a well recognized general purpose weed killer use in grains. Somehow this did not seem right and I asked a neighbor that is a professional weed control expert about using this chemical. His answer was "I don't know what its effect is on corn but I will find out." In the mean time I bought 2-4-D but did not apply it. My friend got back to me with the answer that this chemical would stunt the growth and seriously retard the corn's production. Again it was inspiration that saved me from a costly mistake.

You asked, "What did you do to control the weeds?" Simple I tilled and hoed the weeds until the corn was high enough to fend for itself. This again was a lot of work but it was successful.

It was now time to fertilize the corn. I had a couple of large tanks of fertilizer that had been given to me, but no effective way to apply it other than a hand sprayer. I looked into buying a fertilizer injector for the irrigation system but these units were expensive. Then I got my thinking cap on and asked for a little help. I was inspired to build a fertilizer injector for the irrigation system. This is what I used to build a fertilizer injector.

I started with an old discarded well pressure tank. Took the bottom plate off and turned the tank upside down. I was able to put a piece of pipe to the bottom of the tank and then fill

106

CHARLES L (BUD) EVANS

the tank with fertilizer. The tank was pressurized with air pressure to force the fertilizer out of the tank. I constructed an orifice into the irrigation line. The flow of the fertilizer was controlled by valves and as long as the air pressure in the tank was greater than the pressure of the irrigation system the injector worked just fine. This is how the corn was fertilized.

Next year I am going to get the proper weed spray and apply it through the irrigation system also. The injector system will be refined and improved.

Missing Picture is available in the Kindle Edition.

Now all that was left to do was to water the corn and watch it grow. Watering took about half an hour a day and was an enjoyable experience. Grow it did. Some of the corn grew to over 12 feet tall. Most stocks had two ears of corn and one had six really good sized ears. This corn was amazing.

HARVESTING THE CORN

We were not able to find a mechanical corn picker that we could buy or borrow. So guess what? You guessed it, we picked the corn by hand and that was a lot of work the whole family helped and we got it done the first part of November. It is not all shucked yet (husks removed from the corn ears) but most of it is done. Here is the pile that still needs to be processed.

The next picture shows the corn with the husks still in place. It is work to remove those husks by hand.

You can see all the pictures in the Kindle edition.

This is what the corn looks like in the bin for storage. You notice the old pvc drain pipe with holes drilled in the pipe. This pipe is to provide ventilation to dry the corn and maintain air flow during storage.

As you can see the Lord provided nice ears of corn for our animals.

The next step is how to best provide this feed to our chickens. The proper way to feed corn to chickens is as cracked corn, that is corn that has the kernels broken or ground. We don't have a corn grinder. The Lord provided a grinder in a strange way. A family was moving out of the area and had a lot of stuff to sell. They had this old chipper and shredder for yard wastes to sell. It was a heavy old beast and needed a lot of work. I thought that the price was too high but a still small voice said to buy it. Well I bought it and rebuilt it. Because it is old and heavily built it is perfect for grinding chicken feed. I just throw the corn on the cob in the shredder and it comes out ground chicken feed.

You see this old shredder with some of the chickens we raised this year.

Here is the corn patch after it was picked as you can see this was a pretty large corn field to grow by hand. Well except for the small tractor to till the ground. It is a miracle that this project was ever completed so successfully.

Lord's Corn Patch After Harvest view in Kindle Edition

SUMMARY AND TESTIMONY OF THIS PROJECT

The inspiration for this project began after we had set a goal as a family to grow 50 percent, that's half of our own food this year. With the Lord's help we achieved that goal. This corn project is a major part of that goal. The Lord has blessed us in many ways with his corn patch. The corn patch was not my idea. We are all under direction to grow as much of our own food as possible. I strongly advise everyone to grow as much food for themselves and their families as they can. This applies

CHARLES L (BUD) EVANS

to you whether you are a member of the Church of Jesus Christ of Latterday Saints or not. You still have to eat. Food will become an expensive and scarce commodity in this country if we don't change our ways.

Please remember that the inspiration and direction to plant and care for this corn patch came before a drought in the mid United States was evident. Since the beginning of this project the price of corn in our local feed store has nearly doubled.

Here is what we have obtained from this project to date:

About 2 ton of corn, we have already fed our chickens for three months on home grown corn. We had three or four hens running wild around the place last spring. Those few hens produced about 100 chicks that have grown to maturity as free ranging chickens this year. In all the years that we have raised chickens we have never seen this kind of wild production. What this will net is three dozen hens to lay eggs and the rest in the freezer.

My wife and daughters canned about 100 quarts of corn and put quite a bit in the freezer from this project. The Lord truly blesses us when we keep his commandments.

In summary we have a year's supply of chicken feed and about a year's supply of chicken to eat from this corn patch. With the continual increase in food prices this is a great blessing to our family.

What does all of this mean to you? This means that if you have a will to accomplish something and ask the Lord's help you can do it. It does not mean that things will be just handed to you.

I testify to you that this project was a modern day miracle. The Lord's hand in this successful project was evident at every turn. My greatest blessing was the sure knowledge that the

Lord Jesus Christ will help us to achieve righteous goals. I testify to this in the name of Jesus Christ—AMEN.

CHAPTER 18
ALTERNATIVES TO STANDARD MEDICINE

Why do we need to look at alternative medical treatments?

- There may be a more effective way to treat a condition outside of conventional medical practice.
- Medicines may not always be available from normal distribution channels.
- The Medical and Pharmaceutical industries are some of the most corrupt and price controlling groups.
- Getting an alternative perspective on personal health is a good idea.

How do you find alternative medical information? The best way is to do internet research; there is always information on the net. You will need to research each item that is of interest to you. If you find a substitute for a conventional medicine that you need then do extensive research upon that item. If you have a good relationship with you Medical Doctor then talk it over with him.

Remember that the medical profession is scripted to a very narrow method of dealing with problems. Their basic method of operation is to diagnose a symptom and then look up a drug to treat the symptom. They are not trained to look for causes or ways to change your life style to remove the cause. Some MD's try to treat the causes but they are not well supported by the pharmaceutical companies, after all if you fix the cause you can't sell a lot of drugs to treat the symptoms.

The best example that I have seen is in cancer cures and treatments. There are a lot of supposed cancer cures that might work I don't know. I do know that the Government, American Medical Association and the pharmaceutical companies will not support research to prove or disprove these cancer treatments. The most widely know is the use of cesium chloride to treat cancer. The papers all debunk the cure but no one has done a controlled study to learn the facts about this treatment. The studies that have been conducted certainly did not meet the approved scientific model, however, they show results that are miraculous. The people treated in a couple of the studies that I read were all terminal cancer patients, in other words they had been left to die by the medical profession. Approximately 30% of these folks survived with this treatment. That to me indicates sufficient evidence to fund and conduct research to prove or disprove this treatment and to do the study in an open to the public manner. I do know that if I was diagnosed with extreme cancer I would not have a problem trying one of the alternative treatments. What would I have to lose?

You need to do your own research for alternative medicine and life style changes that may improve your health.

CHARLES L (BUD) EVANS

CHAPTER 19
WHY SHOULD YOU?

This should have been chapter 13 because it is where all the nasty things are discussed that you need to know to develop a WHY you should take action. Your future and that of your family depend upon you taking action today. Your first step should be to make a plan of how you are going to survive in the 21 century.

THE BAD AND NASTY FACTS:

- We are faced with climatic change and we can't do anything about it.
- Our country is governed by drunks at least not by those with our best interest in heart. It is no longer a government of the people, by the people and for the people. Our economy is in the dumpster.
- We do not have a shortage of natural resources including oil and other energy products.
- Greed is a larger part of our life than love of our fellow man.
- Written history has been modified to deceive the common man.
- We could see famine greater than that talked about in the Bible.
- Global warming is a myth. Global cooling may be the reality.
- Freedom will cease to exist in the United States of American in the next 15 years unless we mend our ways.

- We are facing a worldwide food shortage.
- The medical community no longer cares about human beings, only money. For example the local dentist here in Benton City, Washington charges $300.00 for a simple tooth extraction. They have no remorse in telling you that if you can't pay don't bother us. Obamacide is real and working.

CLIMATIC CHANGE

I can't tell you what the climatic change will be where you live but you can bet that it will change. It is probably impossible for anyone to predict what our climate will do in the next 10 to 50 years. It will change and here are some of the reasons.

The earth's axis has changed orientation to the sun by a significant amount. If you can measure this change it is significant to our weather and climatic conditions.

The sun spot cycle appears to be approaching an all time low. This means that solar energy will be reduced.

Due to axis shift, sunspot cycle and alignment of the planets the earth's magnetic shield could be vulnerable to penetration by high energy cosmic particles. This will cause magnetic storms and other unusual events. A good example of this is an unusual lightning storm over the Rattlesnake Mountains of Eastern Washington in late December of 2012. It was not reported any where. I know it happened because I observed it. My guess is that the government suppressed the importance of this event to prevent possible panic of the people. I have interviewed a lot of the "old timers" in this community and they stated these things. 1) We have never had lightning storms in the winter. 2) We only started to hear thunder and see lightning here about 20 years ago. I am not sure how true the se-

114

CHARLES L (BUD) EVANS

cond statement is but when I was teaching school in Mabton, Washington about 1966 I do not remember any thunder storms, just a little rain in the spring and some snow in the winter. The significance of these statements is change is accelerated and we don't know what the change will be.

Here are a few facts to back up these ideas:

The Mayan calendar ended with no significant change or did it? In December of 2012 there was a galactic alignment of planets, sun, and the Milky Way galaxy that could have had a gravitational affect upon on the already shifted earth's axis. My personal opinion is that the real damage will be caused by the effect upon the earth's magnetic shield. This could create holes or passageways for high energy cosmic radiation to enter the space between the magnetic shield and the atmosphere.

In July of 2012 Climatologist Cliff Harris stated:"It remains the opinion of this climatologist that this 7-year cycle of extremes won't peak until at least 2038. We will continue to see long-standing weather records broken worldwide on an accelerated scale."

If this is not climatic change what is it?

The drought of 2012 is now a matter of record rivaling the "dust bowl" days of the 1930's.

During the same time frame central Australia reported frigid temperatures in the low 20 on the Fahrenheit scale. Peru reported temperatures below 12 degree Fahrenheit in areas of generally mild temperatures.

Climatologist Cliff Harris states, "What's ahead weatherwise is anyone's guess. Expect the 'unusual' and you'll undoubtedly be right."

THIS LOOKS LIKE A GOOD REASON TO STORE FOOD TO ME.

115

DO WE HAVE A SHORTAGE OF NATURAL RE-SOURCES?

The answer is no. We have adequate resources for the next 1000 years if we are a little bit prudent in the way that they are used. In his report "The Third Term" Porter Stansberry, of S & A Investment Research defines our petroleum energy reserves. We have plenty. I am not sure that I agree with his analysis that the cost of gasoline and heating fuel will go down. Under the current government and international policies it looks to me like greed will be the factor that sets the price and not supply and demand. In any case having enough oil is not the problem. The problem is government regulation and political profiteering.

We have an ample supply of all the metals that we need to sustain our country if we use them to manufacture finished products in this country.

We need to conserve our greatest resource "We the People." The average Joe on the streets of the United States is just a mark for the established world powers to use to make more money. This is not about countries but rather about private greed and power.

Getting out of debt makes sense even if it requires personal sacrifice.

CHAPTER 20
TIME MANAGEMENT CREATES SUCCESS

INTRODUCTION

I have a confession to make. This started out as a chapter in another book on how to be successful in life. As I grew older it appeared that time management might well be the ultimate key to success. The number of hours that we have in each day is the same for each of us. The same can be said for each week, month, and year. The only unknown is how long we will live. That is not important if we make the most of each hour.

Since I wrote the original chapter on time management several things have come to mind. Most of us with even the best of plans and preparation cannot manage our time on an instant by instant basis.

My recent experience has taught me that focus and how you spend your working time is one of the essentials of success. It is great to have a daily, weekly, monthly and even yearly time management plan complete with goal setting. The rubber meets the road when you attempt to apply these plans. This book will fill that gap and help you with your long term time management goal.

You just asked the question: Why is there a time section in a book about surviving the 21St Century? You never have enough time and unless you utilize what you have you will not be prepared.

TIME MANAGEMENT

What is time management? To understand time management we must first understand what time is. Time in general is defined as the space between two events such as when the sun comes up and when the sun goes down. Time is a quantity that can't be stored or put away for a rainy day. The unique quality of time is that it is the universal equalizer. Rich or poor, smart or not so smart, we all have the same amount of time each day. Each day is made up of 24 hours. This may be measured by the vibrations of an atomic clock or by observing the solar system. No mater how you measure it your 24 hours and is the same as my twenty four hours. The difference comes from what I do with my 24 hours and what you do with your 24 hours.

This goes back to the statement that every action has a consequence. The time spent to achieve a specific consequence is time management. The simplicity of time management is that we get to choose how we will spend our time.

Deciding how to spend your time is the important and most difficult part. If you have specific goals or things that you want to accomplish then you must provide time to accomplish them. You must decide what is most important.

THE THREE P'S

You have seen this section before in the planning area. Read it again here as it is that important. There is one thing that you must do before you can set goals that facilitate management of your time. That thing is to develop a life plan that will enable you to accomplish those things in life that are most important to you. GOALS

CHARLES L (BUD) EVANS

In order to manage your time you must know what is important and that is where goals enter the picture. To effectively manage your time you must have an end point in mind.

This brings up the question: What are goals? A goal is the very essence of life. Without a goal for your life and the sub goals that go with it you are like a cork in a pond. You are pushed this way and that way maybe you will end up on the other side of the pond or you might get washed over the spillway.

As I sit in my chair thinking about goal setting I realize that it is an area that I have not defined clearly for myself or written a way for others to achieve great goal setting. This is not an easy task. Goal setting starts with looking deep into your soul to discover what it is that makes you go. The preliminary to goal setting is development of a life plan. This is when things get tough.

My personal opinion is to look into ourselves and see what we really want out of life. Most people seem to want the same things in the core of their being. For most it is something like this; Family and companionship, financial security, meaningful work or service, and leisure activities that are meaningful to the individual.

I will share my core values with you. My great passions in life are:

- Family
- Service
- Fixing things
- Gardening
- Learning and writing.

My goals from these are fairly simple but not so easy to obtain. My passion for my family breaks down into many areas. Some are:

- Financial
- Friendship and relationships
- Legacy
- Tradition

The other areas can be broken down into many smaller pieces also. One similar point in all of these personal passions is a financial piece. Everything that we do must be funded in some manner and that leads us to financial planning and managing our money. In order to do this we must have our goals in order.;

Many people would call the statement of our life a mission statement. Yes, I have one that took me three years to write. That was many years ago and it has changed little since. My mission statement is in reality a statement of my core values and how I will apply them in my life. I am not going to attempt to tell you how to write a mission statement in this document. There are volumes written on how to write a mission statement.

I spent three years writing a mission statement. This is my guiding document. It provides the ground rules that I use to develop my goals and to determine what constitutes success for me. A couple of good books to start with about writing a mission statement are 7 HABITS OF HIGH EFFECTIVE PEOPLE and PUT FIRST THINGS FIRST by Steven Covey. Not only will these two books get you on the correct path to create a mission statement but will also provide great insight into living a better and happier live. After all isn't that what success is all about?

CHARLES L (BUD) EVANS

You have decided what is important in your life—good. Now it is time to write goals for each area and to break the major goals down into sub goals. In order to accomplish this task we must define the parts of a goal. A goal contains these parts.

A definite and defined statement of the goal: Success depends upon how well the goal is defined. This must be a written statement.

- The goal must include a brief but complete description.
- The goal must explain how the goal will be obtained.
- The goal must include a definite due date.

There is another side to the goal thing. Many people think that achievement of a goal is success. This may not be the truth.

There are almost as many definitions of success as there are people writing them. The most common definition is that of a journey. Some have stated it like this "Success is the continual realization of worthwhile goals." This is a good behavioral based definition but it raises the question, "What are worthwhile goals?" A worthwhile goal to me may not be worthwhile to you. Eradication of all Piranhas in the Amazon: would not be a worthwhile goal to me. The point is that each of us must decide what is important in our lives.

There are strings attached to what we want to achieve. It must not be harmful to humanity and it must provide a service to others. Many of the great figures of history have accomplished goals that were not for the good of mankind. The checks and balances of God and the universe tend to level out these low spots. For continuous happiness we must not violate the rights of others. You have to look deep into your soul to

121

determine what is right and wrong in any situation. There are no hard rules for all cases.

The concept of happiness and success seem to be linked in some way. All of the achievement (goal accomplishment) in the world is not of any value if you are not happy in getting to the goal. When a goal is achieved it does not automatically mean that we are happy and successful. For a lot of us achieving a goal leaves a feeling of emptiness. The accomplishment of a goal always raises the question. "Where do I go from Here?"

I wrote the paragraphs above over ten years ago. I still have not created a good definition for success. I can now tell you what it is not. It is not the size of your bank account, the number of cars that you own or the value of your house. All of these things contribute to your material well being. They do not in themselves make you happy or create great joy in your life. Great personal power is not success. Many people believe that personal power and the accumulated things of life create a successful person. I disagree with the idea that things and power define success. I have never met a man on his death bed that wished he had spent more time making money. Most people preparing to meet their maker talk about family and how they treated their wife. They talk about family and what a mess they made of certain situation. These comments all lead me to believe that true success and joy come from the relationship of our soul and the rest of God's Children.

The man that raised several children to be successful adults (they don't have to be perfect) and has remained good friends with his children is more successful than the man that has millions in the bank and his children are waiting for him to die so that they can fight over his money. Wealth in itself is not wrong but it takes a great man to handle great wealth in an honest and upstanding manner.

CHARLES L (BUD) EVANS

Each of us must define success in our own terms. If you feel that success should make you happy then you must also define what "happy" means to you. This seems like an endless loop but it is not. Happy is only one component of success.

PRIORITIZING YOUR ACTIONS.

Your actions should be prioritized to lead to the goal that you wish to achieve. Everyone needs to have life time goals. This should be discussed in your mission statements and your mission statement should include you ultimate goals. My recommended method of prioritization is to do it on a weekly basis. Daily is too short and monthly is too long to keep track of.

Prioritization must reflect the importance of each item on your task list. I use the A,B,C method.

A = Important and urgent=

B = Important not urgent

C = not important and not urgent.

D= A total waste of time

Where do these categories come from? My first observation of this method was in Stephen Covey's book, **7 HABITS OF HIGHLY EFFECTIVE PEOPLE** . I don't think that they originated with Covey as I have seen similar grids in other places. In any case, an adaption of the grid is included.

This grid is the central thought in all time management methods. The individual must remain in quadrant I and quadrant II. The best application of this method is to remain in quadrant II. This is not always possible as some urgent and important issues always are present in our live. The more that we are in quadrant II the less stress we have in our live.

123

Quadrants III and IV should be avoided like bad germs. Most of the items in these two quadrants bring little productive results and not that much pleasure either.

Time management: Tips to reduce stress and improve productivity

Effective time management is a primary means to a less stressful life. These practices can help you reduce your stress and reclaim your personal life.

By Mayo Clinic staff

"Do you find yourself overwhelmed by the number and complexity of projects you have that need to be completed at work each day? Do you often feel the day flies by without your devoting the necessary attention to each assignment because other tasks keep landing on your desk, co-workers interrupt you with questions or you can't get it all organized?

You probably know that effective time management will help you get more done each day. It has important health benefits, too. By managing your time more wisely, you can minimize stress and improve your quality of life.

But how do you get back on track when organizational skills don't come naturally? To get started, choose one of these strategies, try it for two to four weeks and see if it helps. If it does, consider adding another one. If not, try a different one.

Plan each day. Planning your day can help you accomplish more and feel more in control of your life.

Write a to-do list, putting the most important tasks at the top. Keep a schedule of your daily activities to minimize conflicts and last-minute rushes.

Prioritize your tasks. Time-consuming but relatively unimportant tasks can consume a lot of your day. Prioritizing tasks will ensure that you spend your time and energy on those that are truly important to you.

124

CHARLES L (BUD) EVANS

Say no to nonessential tasks. Consider your goals and schedule before agreeing to take on additional work.

Delegate: Take a look at your to-do list and consider what you can pass on to someone else.

Take the time you need to do a quality job. Doing work right the first time may take more time upfront, but errors usually result in time spent making corrections, which takes more time overall.

Break large, time-consuming tasks into smaller tasks. Work on them a few minutes at a time until you get them all done.

Practice the 10-minute rule. Work on a dreaded task for 10 minutes each day. Once you get started, you may find you can finish it.

Evaluate how you're spending your time. Keep a diary of everything you do for three days to determine how you're spending your time. Look for time that can be used more wisely. For example, could you take a bus or train to work and use the commute to catch up on reading? If so, you could free up some time to exercise or spend with family or friends.

Limit distractions. Block out time on your calendar for big projects. During that time, close your door and turn off your phone, pager and e-mail.

Get plenty of sleep, have a healthy diet and exercise regularly. A healthy lifestyle can improve your focus and concentration, which will help improve your efficiency so that you can complete your work in less time.

Take a time management course. If your employer offers continuing education, take a time management class. If your workplace doesn't have one, find out if a local community college, university or community education program does.

Take a break when needed. Too much stress can derail your attempts at getting organized. When you need a break, take one. Take a walk. Do some quick stretches at your work-station. Take a day of vacation to rest and re-energize". End of quote from Mayo Clinic.

One way to accomplish more is to use what I call the A + B + C rule. This is a very simple rule. Do one thing at a time. If you have three projects to complete it will take three times as long to complete them if you work on one and switch over to another. There is no logic as to why things work this way, they just do. If you start project A work on it until it is finished, your day is done, or you run out of materials or information that you must wait for others to supply. There is one other factor that you must consider, If you get burned out and hit a brick wall with the project. Take some time away from that particular project. This does not necessarily mean to start on B, however, that can be an option but probably not the best option for the same is true for C.

Let us take a moment and look at where we are in all of this. You have a lot of information about planning and develop-ing plan and goals. Your next question could be this. I don't have all of those things done and probably won't accomplish them for some time, so what do I do in the mean time. Believe it or not I have an answer for you. This is a problem that all of us face every week in our lives. Here the key word is week.

Let's take a moment and imagine a large glass jar sitting in front of us. This jar represents the time that we have in a week. The question is, how do we use the space in the jar to accom-plish the most in that week. Let's represent our major tasks for the week as large rocks that will just barely fit through the mouth of the jar. First we put in those major tasks. Is our jar full, well not exactly, as there is still space around the rocks. Those rocks represent the things that must be done in the next week. If there is still some time left in the week as represented

CHARLES L (BUD) EVANS

by the empty space in the jar what do we do with it? We have developed a weekly plan with our major rocks noted. What can rocks be broken down to, yup you guessed it—pebbles and sand. The pebbles and sand are the less important items. One mistake you must not make. The size of the project does not necessarily determine its priority.

A high priority item might be to put gas in your car. This probably won't take a lot of time, just a lot of cash. The consequence of not doing this task is a long walk. These big rocks are based upon importance not amount of time, the cost or the size of the task. This is where you use the prioritization grid. Stay in quadrants I and II.

You have prioritized your tasks for a week now you can manage your time on a daily basis.

The illustration that you see is based upon what Dr. Covey teaches in the 7 Habits book. You can develop your own weekly template with a little effort. I stole the one I use out of a workbook from Dr. Covey.

After you have developed your long and short term time management plan, the plan must be applied in a doable manner. This usage plan must take into account the human aspect of focus. You have a weekly plan developed. Take this plan and estimate the amount of time each task will take. Break those tasks down into about 30 minute segments for each day if you can. Learning to do this takes practice and is never an exact science. (I still fail miserably at this task).

The average human attention span is 30 minutes or less.

Adequate rest periods are essential for your best work.

Length of work periods need to match the way that the human mind works.

Multi-tasking is a myth for effective and efficient work.

If these things are true, then how can I apply these principles to my time management? These ideas can be easily applied. I use a timer to time my actions. The timer that I use is on my computer it is called the Action Enforcer. This is not a free program. It can be found at this link. http://nanacast.com/vp/96244/234316/

My method of work focus time management is an off shoot of the Pomodoro Technique. The book that describes this technique is available from Amazon.com.(http://www.amazon.com/gp/product/1934356506/ref=as_li_s s_tl?ie=UTF8&camp=1789&creative=390957&creativeASIN=19 34356506&linkCode=as2&tag=rattlemountae-20).Here is how I use the technique. The Pomodoro Technique follows an old rule, If you want to eat an elephant take many small bites. To apply this technique your work project must be broken down in to elements or steps that you believe will take two hours or less. If they will take more than this then find the smaller steps necessary to complete the element you are working on. The working time is broken down into 25 minute segments with a 5 minute break every 25 minutes. At the end of 4 of these work segments you take a 30 minute break. This creates six of these rounds in an eight hour day. For reasons that I don't understand after a day using this method compared to a conventional approach to work I am less tired and usually have gotten more accomplished.

I have a small auto repair business on the side. This technique even works for these types of projects. Sometimes I have to stretch the 25 minutes a little if I am in the middle of something that cannot be stopped. For the most part the method works rather well in nearly all situations.

CHARLES L (BUD) EVANS

SUMMARY

In summary time management is all about bossing yourself. To repeat myself the greatest lesson anyone ever taught me came from my father. When I was about 12 years old I forgot to do some chore at home. My Father said to me, "You will never amount to a damn until you learn to boss yourself." That is time management in a nutshell, learn to boss yourself. This is the central key to all of the other natural laws. Time Management is a mindset. If this isn't clear, think about it.

CHAPTER 21
HOME SECURITY PLAN

Everyone needs some sort of home security plan. Mine is simple a son-in-law from the National Guard with PTSC from Iraq. The backup plan is another son-in-law that is a trigger happy security guard with PTSC. The back up to these is two German Sheppards, an Akaka and a mutt lab.

We are constructing 6 foot chain link fence around the place as rapidly as we can afford it. We also are constructing a 6 foot used tire fence filled with dirt around the entrance drive way.

There are 5 security cameras hooked up to a standalone computer.

Our best security plan is the network of neighbors that live here. We help one another and watch each other's back.

I can't tell you what you need as I don't know where you live. You must do your own research. I can tell you that you need a home security plan. One of my favorite places for information like this is the offthegridnews.com.

Here are few thoughts from an article that I purchased.

"INTRODUCTION TO HOME SECURITY

Most people fail to see that they could be the next victim of fire, burglary, violence, etc. The fact is none of us is safe from fire, crime, carbon monoxide poison, etc. Health is a great example to use, which can help you see that no one is exceptional to the rules of life. No matter how healthy a person is, one day he will die, or fall ill. After all life is a life threatening disease you can't get out alive.

The facts must hit you in the face before you can see that home security is important, since you could be the next victim. Nowadays, the world revolves around surviving. Each day a home is threatened by burglary, fire, carbon monoxide, terrorism, violence, crimes, etc. At any given moment, reality could make you the next victim.

In the face of danger, you must learn to follow rules. The rules state that if your home is in danger, the first thing you must do is dial 911. But, when do you dial 911. Where do you dial 911? We must find answers to those questions before we can follow the rules. What do you do if 911 is busy, your fire department is all out on other calls or your police department is working a riot?

All day long, you will read information informing you about home security systems. Each article you read tells you what you get for the price, and how the system can help save your life. What authors do not tell you is that the world is filled with many issues, that not one single home security system can provide you the protection you'll need to survive.

You need to develop your own security plan to cover many different scenarios. Only you can do that. You should have a fire escape plan that is practiced with your family. If members of your family have life threatening medical conditions you should have a plan of what to do if something goes wrong.

What I'm going to tell you will help you decide on your home security system that benefits to, as well as steps you will need to take to protect your home, car, computer, etc.

Why Need a Home Security System?

The world's statistics for criminals is increasing, we all strive to feel safe in our home.. According to statistics, homes are broken into each day, and most homes are violated while the family is on vacation, or away from their home. Most criminals

132

CHARLES L (BUD) EVANS

would rather get in and get out, rather than face potential risks of capture or identification.

A home security system, could significantly reduce the odds of your home being burglarized. You can find a wide selection of home security devices on line. The devices offer you a feature, such as push button call. You merely push a single button that will activate the system and call the police and/or fire department for you. The push buttons offer the advantage that a live voice will respond to the push of one button. Check out Intercom Devices to learn more about such features.

Home security systems are easy to install nowadays. Ultimately, you can purchase wireless kits, which you can install on your own. Be sure to read the manual carefully to make sure the device is installed properly. Don't forget to test your system regularly, dust, and replace parts as needed.

The world is moving toward disaster; be prepared to save your family. Home security includes disaster recovery. Your home plans to escape fire, burglary, carbon monoxide, etc, you should also set up with a backup, or disaster recovery plan. The plans will help you get back on your feet quickly.

ADDITIONAL HOME SECURITY TIPS:

Today, the world is revolving around chaos. Everyday a home is threatened by terrorism, violence, crimes, etc. The first thing you should do if your home is in jeopardy is call 911. If possible, ask the authorities what you need to do first to protect your family. (People tend to act out irrationally at times, for this reason document any conversations you have with the law) Make no exceptions, the law can be your best friend or worst enemy, therefore record all conversations you incur with authorities.

Next, you want to write a floor plan. The floor plan should be a drawing of every room in your home. Make sure that you outline two ways to escape all rooms in your home. You can practice drills to keep the family prepared.

FINDING THE RIGHT HOME SECURITY SYSTEM

Finding home security depends on you, where you live, and what you expect. If you want ultimate home security, you can max out by taking extra precautions, as well as installing proper security systems. Realize that life does not promise us total security; therefore, you want to focus on max security that you budget will allow. What type of neighborhood do you live in?

Do you live in a high crime area?

Is your area covered by adequate law enforcement?

Do you feel safe in your neighborhood?

Knowing what type of neighborhood you live in can help you make a good decision.

HOW CAN I CHOOSE THE RIGHT SECURITY SYSTEM?

There are a variety of home security systems available. Your market research will help decide which type of system you need. The types of home security systems include warning signs and decals, remote monitoring, wireless security, smoke and fire detectors, CO Alarms, video surveillance, voice dialers, security cameras, security alarm system, environmental sensors, dummy cameras, driveway alarms, voice intercoms, sirens and strobe lights, etc.

How can I learn what the security devices can do to secure my home? You can go online to learn more about the products available.

CHARLES L (BUD) EVANS

SECURITY CAMERAS AND RECORDERS

Security cameras include the handheld devices. The cameras work to protect your home and office by enabling you to view your child in a separate room. Your home will have around the clock monitoring, which includes each room. A few of the devices offer you audio and visual surveillance capabilities.

The GX series is a portable unit, which makes it possible to watch activities in all areas of your home on a 2.4 Gigahertz system. The high-resolution camera has an integrated microphone that enables you to listen over a rotating small color LCD screen. The screen will rotate providing you optimal views at various angles. The security cameras are usable in home, office, daycares, stores, etc. The cameras today feature small screens on a crisp imaging device. Security cams may offer you a range of over 250 feet on a clear screen. Cameras today feature rotating screens that support other cameras. Many have integrated microphones, which enable you to hear up to 100 feet or more. Few cameras operate from a number of infrared LED, which allows you to see and hear in the night hours. The cameras will connect to DVR's, VCR, and TVs. In addition, you have automatic and manual switching capabilities between cameras, as well as color adjusting abilities. A few cameras operate on battery power.

My favorite security cam is the Teddy Bear. This handsome feller will sit anywhere you choose, and will hide a camera beneath his fur. You can cuddy with him when the cam is not in use. Inside Mr. Teddy Bear is a small wireless camera that produces color. The bear will store up to 2.4 Gigahertz of footage, while spying with his eye. The bear will help you monitor your child in separate rooms, without the child aware of your action. Teddy has an eight infrared LED, which enables you to see in the dark without turning on the lights. You have receivers, which connect to your DVR, TV, or VCR. The camera works from battery, and can easily be placed in areas out of sight.

Decals and warning signs are as effective as dummy cameras. You post signs on your doors and windows alerting unwelcome visitors that you have an alarm system installed in your home. Even if you do not have a home security system installed, the intention is to deceive criminals. "

CHAPTER 22
THE ULTIMATE DISASTER

What is the ultimate disaster? I think that this is always in the eyes of the beholder. When any disaster strikes us we tend to think that it is the ultimate disaster. I am including a link here to a web site on survival that really impresses me. The owner has some things to sell but has done an excellent job on his survival guide. http://www.lastalive.com

Now back to the ultimate disaster. Each of us must prepare for and define the ultimate disaster. Here is a list of a few of the ultimate disasters that I could face.

Nuclear accident

Earthquake

Wildfire

Government/Monetary collapse

Floods

Drought

Civil War

Dictatorship

Cancer

Health issues

Loss of a Loved One

We live within 10 miles of a nuclear power plant. It has been said that anything created by man can fail. I am not worried about a nuclear accident from this power plant. I know that the safety systems are the best that can be built and I know the folks that run the power plant. Could it survive a terrorist attack, more than likely? Therefore I am not preparing for a nuclear disaster from that plant.

Earthquake is a big item today as we have had an increase in the number of earthquakes and their severity in recent years. I really don't know how to prepare for an earthquake. Our method of preparation is built in to our standard live plan and survival plan. Where we live a tent for shelter in one of our open fields would probably be the best survival plan. The recovery plan for an earthquake is best based upon the damage done and the time require for normal services to be restored. An earthquake survival plan definitely requires a way to maintain your food storage and animal life. This is a difficult plan to construct and depends entirely on where you live or where you are when the quake occurred.

Wildfire: This is the one that can happen to us any summer. In 2000 we had a wildfire the originated on Hanford Nuclear Reservation from a car wreck. This is one of those times when dependence upon 911 was not a great thing. The Department of Energy had requisitioned all of the fire fighting equipment in Eastern Washington to fight the Hanford Fire and the fire got away from the Hanford Fire Department. It was driven by a 50 to 60 mile per hour wind toward Benton City from Department of Energy land. All of the firefighting equipment was either on the Hanford Reservation or at Ki-Be High School. The fire management team controlled by the Department of Energy would not release any of the equipment to fight the wildfire as it left the Hanford Reservation and began to burn private property. I have personally interviewed several firefighters that said two or three of those 40 to 50 fire trucks that were available could have stop the fire or prevented most of the loss of eleven homes and over 100 out buildings.

This is why you need to have your own plans incase Big Brother ignores you. My personal loss was over $500,000.

CHARLES L (BUD) EVANS

Let's discuss government or monetary collapse as they will probably both happen at the same time. That is when your personal, family, and neighborhood survival plans will be very important. You will need to provide your own food and water for your family and help your neighbors too. This could go on for a year or more before a stable government and money system is established. This will happen if we do not fix our way of life that requires us to be dependent entirely upon others and the government. Our government is so far in debt that bankruptcy or a collapse of the monetary system is inevitable. How does a government go bankrupt, its monetary system collapses and hyper inflation takes over? You better be good at barter and have good skills to trade for the items you will need to survive. Get your year's supply of food.

Floods are hard to prepare for but if you live in a 100 year flood plain then you should develop a plan for yourself. There are many on line resources and FEMA has a lot of information available.

Drought and how you prepare for it depends upon where you live. We live in an area with less than 7 inches of rainfall annually. Yup, it is a desert in Eastern Washington. This requires irrigation for anything that we grow. We have pressurized water from the Benton Irrigation District, however the cost is greater than what you can produce and get paid for your labor. The problem is that if government systems collapse we won't have irrigation water. Our plan is to drill deep enough water wells to provide for our gardens at least and have a solar electrical system to pump the water. Make your own drought survival plan. We will see increasing drought for a few years in the United States.

Civil War is a possibility if many of these other factors happen. I can't tell you how to be prepared for civil war other than to stick with your basic survival plan.

One of the causes or aftermaths of civil war is a dictatorship. We have a president that is power hungry and has no sense of what is right and wrong. He could well use any collapse to set himself up as a dictator.

Cancer is a large health issue in the world today. There are 19 documented cures for cancer with reasonable research to back them up since 1941. The medical profession or pharmaceutical companies have not done the research to discredit them or to substantiate their effectiveness.

CHARLES L (BUD) EVANS

CHAPTER 23
PUT TOGETHER A BUG OUT KIT

A bug out kit may also be called a 72 hour kit. It purpose is for you and your family to be able to survive nearly anywhere for 72 hours without any outside help. This also gives you time to figure what your current resources are and what you must do to survive in the future.

When a disaster strikes your community emergency services and government agencies may not be able to respond to your IMMEDIATE NEEDS. Their buildings, equipment, personnel, communications, and mobility may be severely hampered by the event. They will be overwhelmed.

Experts warn that you should be prepared to be on your own for a minimum of **three days** after a disaster. One of the most important elements of this preparedness is the 72-hour kit for your home. The contents of this kit will vary, but in every case it should contain the things you need to survive for three days on your own.

Your home 72-hour kit should contain at least the following items:

- One gallon of water per person per day. This means at least three gallons of water per person.
- Sufficient non-perishable food for three days. Ideally, these foods will be lightweight and high in energy. If you pack canned foods, remember a can opener!
- Prescription and non-prescription medications. Include a spare set of glasses, if you need them.
- Battery powered portable radio. This may be your only source of information during a disaster.

- First aid kit. The small camping kits work well. Remember to get enough supplies for the number of people who may be using them.
- Personal hygiene items.
- Clothing and bedding. A spare pair of socks and a space saver blanket would be a minimum.
- Special items such as baby needs or contact lens supplies, etc.
- Personal comfort items. Books, games, personal electronics, etc.
- Remember, this is only a bare bones kit. You can add things to this list that you or your family will need. The list that follows will give you an idea of where to start. It is a stolen list and I do not know the original author however it is quite good.
- FIRST AID SUPPLIES
- Adhesive bandages, various sizes
- 5 " x 9 " sterile dressing
- Conforming roller gauze bandage
- Triangular bandages
- 3 " x 3 " sterile gauze pads
- 4 " x 4 " sterile gauze pads
- Roll 3 " cohesive bandage
- Germicidal hand wipes or waterless, alcohol based
- hand sanitizer
- Antiseptic wipes
- Medical grade, non-
- latex gloves
- Adhesive tape, 2 " width
- Antibacterial ointment
- Cold pack
- Scissors (small, personal), tweezers

142

- Assorted sizes of safety pins
- Cotton balls, sunscreen
- First aid manual
- Non Prescription and Prescription Medicine
- MEDICAL KIT SUPPLIES
- Aspirin and non-aspirin pain reliever
- Anti-diarrhea medication
- Antacid (for stomach upset)
- Laxative
- Prescriptions
- Extra eyeglasses/contact lenses
- SANITATION AND HYGIENE SUPPLIES
- Washcloth and small towel
- Towelettes and soap
- Tooth paste, toothbrush
- Shampoo, comb, and brush
- Deodorants
- Razor, shaving cream
- Lip balm, insect repellent
- Feminine supplies
- Heavy-duty plastic garbage bags and ties for personal sanitation uses and toilet paper
- Toilet paper
- EQUIPMENT AND TOOLS
- Portable, battery-powered radio or wind-up
- NOAA Weather Radio
- Flashlight (wind-up) and/or extra batteries
- Waterproof matches or in waterproof container
- Manual can opener
- Mess kit or paper cups, plates, and plastic utensils
- Multi-purpose tool,
- Sugar, salt, and pepper

- Duct tape, whistle, work gloves
- Paper, pens, and pencils
- Needles and thread
- Battery-operated travel alarm clock
- Re-sealable plastic bags
- FOOD AND WATER
- Water (4 pints)
- Ready-to-eat meats, fruits, and vegetables
- Canned or boxed juices, milk, and soup
- High-energy foods such as peanut butter, jelly, low-sodium crackers, granola bars, and trail mix
- Special foods for persons on special diets
- Cookies, hard candy
- Cereals and powdered milk
- Clothes and Bedding Supplies
- Clothes and bedding supplies
- Complete change of clothes (3 day supply)
- Sturdy shoes or boots
- Rain gear, hat, sunglasses
- Blankets/sleeping bags and camp pillows
- DOCUMENTS AND KEYS
- Personal identification
- Cash and coins (mimum $100.00), credit cards
- Extra set of house keys and car keys
- Copy of birth certificate, marriage certificate
- Copy of driver's license, social security cards
- Copy of passports, wills and deeds
- Insurance papers, immunization records
- Bank and credit card account numbers
- Emergency contact list and phone numbers
- Map of the area & phone numbers of places you could go. This is important and also notify someone in your

CHARLES L (BUD) EVANS

church or government where they can reach you if
you leave your home.

This is a good place to start now you must make up your
own Bug-Out-Bag.

CHAPTER 24
SUMMARY PRIOR TO
CHAPTER 13

We have covered a lot of territory in this document. It still is not a complete guide to surviving. It is the duty of every individual and family to take this basic information and apply the information to their personal situation. The original offering of this book will be in kindle format, however, if you will sign up for our newsletter at http://self-sufficientliving.net and include a copy of your Amazon payment receipt I well send you the PDF file of the book. You really need a hard copy to put with your 72 hour kit.

We are facing extreme change in climate most anywhere on the planet. That is a given, what it will be is probably an unknown. This is a good reason to store food and fuel to ride out the small or large disasters as they happen.

We need to be concerned about those things that we can change. We can change how we spend our money and control our debt. Each of us can develop a plan for getting out of debt.

When we make political choices, in other words vote; look for those candidates that seem to be connected to what America was in years past. I think a saying from one of the major religions should be applied to our country, "Be of the world but not part of the world."

My personal opinion is that we are facing several years of severe drought in this country and perhaps for most of the planet. The Russian people recognize this and served notice on the US Government that if they have another drought year like 2012, they will sell no grain to the U.S.

I wonder how this works with President Obama's idea that we don't need strategic grain reserves. He sold the last of our strategic grain reserves in July of 2010. His reasoning was that since we have lots of money we can always buy it off the open market. The question is will there be any available.

When it comes to being hungry, people will do most anything to eat. Rumor has it that the US Government strategic threat analysis groups have been analyzing the threat of a hungry populous to the political government. The conclusion is to try to contain them in the cities and let them starve or kill themselves. This does not sound like a government of the people, by the people and for the people to me.

My conclusion is that personal preparedness is our only chance at survival. The check list will get you started on the road to survival. It's not about guns and ammunition but about food and water.

The United States Government has purchased about a billion rounds of hollow point ammunition. This is against the Geneva Convention so it must be for use on US soil.

CHARLES L (BUD) EVANS

CHAPTER 25
CHAPTER 13 WHAT YOU CAN EXPECT

This chapter is titled chapter 13 for a reason and it is not because it come after another number. This chapter contains either the best luck this country could ever have or the greatest nightmare. It is meant to scare you but not to debilitate you. The whole purpose of this chapter is to force you to take action to protect yourself and your family.

This is the update of the book SURVIVE THE 21ST CENTURY. Much of the material in this book is taken from that book with modifications and a reformat of the book. Today's date is October 1, 2013. As you already know this is the day that the Government of the United States of America shut down because of Obamacide i.e. Obamacare. The real issue with this legislation was not about medical care but rather the other things that are in that bill. The other things in that bill are why a President that wants to establish a dictatorship in this country would not compromise to maintain the status quo of our county. The Obamacide act removes most personal freedom from this country and gives the government power to seize your assets without due process for any medical bills or alleged medical expenses without recourse. This alone should spur you to implement as much of this book as you can.

Last year we saw a major shortage of grain in this country. It is rumored that President Obama received a letter from the Russian Governments that stated that they would have no grain for sale in 2013. Did you know that the greatest agricultural producing country in the world imports a large share of its grain? We have had unusual weather causing crop failures throughout these United States in 2013. Some examples of this are the unseasonal rains that destroyed a big chunk of the grain crop in Montana. A local example is a wind storm two days before this was written that destroyed about 1000 acres of crops not twenty miles from where I live at least 400 acres of this crop was corn. California has a virus that destroyed most of their pepper crop. This I know because these companies are in Eastern Washington as I write trying to buy hot pepper to make up for the loss. These sound like small things but if they are applied worldwide and the indication are that they are happening worldwide then we are looking at food shortages and a hungry planet. Not caused by over population but mismanagement of our resources to give a few power and money over others. If you doubt that we import a large part of our food then do this look at where the food you buy in the grocery store is grown. If it specifically is not label made or grown in the USA, then it is imported.

Did you know that a large part of our corn in the USA is diverted to make fuel for our vehicles rather than to feed people and livestock for meat. The irony of this process is that it takes more energy to produce the fuel from the alcohol than it would to burn oil products. In a report titled, The Third Term Porter Stansberry states that we have no oil shortage in this country. He goes on to say that we have enough undeveloped and oil fields being explored to make this country the Mecca of energy for the world.

Porter Stansberry state in the report and I quote. "Using vast new powers, I believe Obama will:

- Greatly increase the size of the Fed's quantitative easing, leading to massive increases to inflation.
- Seize control of the entire 401K retirement system,

150

CHARLES L (BUD) EVANS

forcing Americans to buy more of our government's risky debt.

- Implement vast new taxes across our economy, as they have already done with the health care program and which they will do next by implementing a national sales tax.
- Continue to expand the welfare rolls by record amounts, buying still more votes, more power and setting the stage for a third Obama term (something I'll explain in this letter.)
- Reshape our foreign policy, drawing American into partnerships with dictators and socialists around the world"

You can see that, two years later, as this report was written in late 2010 and early 2011, that many of these things have come to pass. There is an old saying, "Control the food and you control the people."

This looks like a good reason to implement a home security plan and a food storage plan.

To many, it looks like we are moving closer and closer to a revolution. That is the last thing that I want to see as it will not solve the problem for the eternities.

The Obamacide, i.e. the Obomacare plan contain the language necessary to seize the countries' retirement system. Your 401K is gone, kiss it good bye as the government will use it the same way that they did Social Security fund many years ago.

I realize that we can't change most of these things but we can be prepared to survive them. The advice in this book will go a long way to helping you to survive if you apply it. If you grow your own food you are fairly safe from added taxes and inflation.

The Office of Home Land Security has purchased close to a billion rounds of hollow point bullets. The purpose of these munitions is to keep people in the cities and let they burn themselves out.

WHAT DO I THINK WILL HAPPEN FOR THE NEXT 20 YEARS?

My prediction is that the United States government will survive and that President Obama will not be able to complete his plans to create this country as a socialist dictatorship.

The economy is going to be the factor that brings about a revolution in this country. I do not expect it to be a civil war. I expect these things to happen.

- 2013 December or January 2014 we will see the beginning of inflation.
- 2014 through 2016 or 2017 inflation will continue and be termed hyper inflation. The greatest price increases will be in food.
- About 2018 we will begin a process of deflation that will continue for 10 to 15 years. This period will come to be called a depression. This is the period of "shake out" when the world equalizes to prepare for the next 250 year growth and change cycle.

What can you do? The best plan of action is the one outlined in this book. I believe that if you implement this plan you and your family will survive and prosper.

CHAPTER 26
RESOURCES

Emergency Preparedness 101 this is web site of a friend of mine that has a good back ground in preparedness. It is worth a look. www.emergencypreparedness101.net

Federal Emergency Management Agency (FEMA) This is a good site with lots of information. http://www.fema.gov/

Mother Earth News is a magazine and web site that I have followed for years. Mother Earth News

Many books and other resources at this site. Bud's Free Books http://budsfreebooks.com/

Lots of information here: Self Sufficient Living, Living Self Sufficient In the 21st Century. http://www.self-sufficientliving.net/

Great book on Kindle about an old dog. OLD ROVER MY BEST FRIEND, available on Amazon.

Heirloom Garden Seeds. Baker Creek Heirloom Seeds. http://www.rareseeds.com/

The Church of Jesus Christ of Latter-Day Saints Provident Living web site. http://providentliving.org/?lang=eng

Another great book on emergency preparedness: THE PRE-PARED FAMILY, available from Amazon.

Drive your Car 300,000 miles; DUMMIES GUIDE TO A 300,000 MILE CAR (CARS) You can get this on Amazon.com

NOTES

Every book like this needs a place for you to save your dis-
covered information. That is what the next few pages are for.

156

CHARLES L (BUD) EVANS

158

CHARLES L (BUD) EVANS

160

CHARLES L (BUD) EVANS

CHARLES L (BUD) EVANS

164

CHARLES L (BUD) EVANS

167

CHARLES L (BUD) EVANS

www.ingramcontent.com/pod-product-compliance
Lightning Source LLC
Chambersburg PA
CBHW072250270326

41930CB00010B/2333